Buildings, Clothing, and Art

EMORY DEAN KEOKE

KAY MARIE PORTERFIELD

Facts On File, Inc.

Buildings, Clothing, and Art

Copyright © 2005 by Emory Dean Keoke and Kay Marie Porterfield
Maps on pages 122–132 © 2005 by Carl Waldman
Maps on pages 44, 133–134 © 2005 by Facts On File, Inc.

Facts On File, Inc.
132 West 31st Street
New York NY 10001

Library of Congress Cataloging-in-Publication Data
Keoke, Emory Dean.
   American Indian contributions to the world. Buildings, clothing, and art / Emory Dean Keoke and Kay Marie Porterfield.
      v. cm.
   Includes bibliographical references and index. Contents: Introduction—Houses of snow and houses of wood—Houses of fiber and bark and houses of hide—Houses of earth and houses of stone—Public buildings and cities—Clothing from hides—Clothing from fiber—Wearable art—Baskets and pottery—Painting and sculpture.
   ISBN 0-8160-5394-4 (hc)
   1. Indian architecture—Juvenile literature. 2. Indian art—Juvenile literature. 3. Indians—Clothing—Juvenile literature. [1. Indian architecture. 2. Indian art. 3. Indians—Clothing. 4. Indians of North America. 5. Indians of Central America. 6. Indians of South America.] I. Porterfield, Kay Marie. II. Title.
E59.A67K46 2005
704.03'97—dc22   2003019474

Facts On File books are available at special discounts when purchased in bulk quantities for businesses, associations, institutions, or sales promotions. Please call our Special Sales Department in New York at (212) 967-8800 or (800) 322-8755.

You can find Facts On File on the World Wide Web at http://www.factsonfile.com

Text design by Erika K. Arroyo
Cover design by Cathy Rincon
Maps by Sholto Ainslie

Printed in the United States of America

VB FOF 10 9 8 7 6 5 4 3 2 1

This book is printed on acid-free paper.

For our grandchildren:
Jason Keoke, Gwendolyn Z. McPherson,
Matthew Geboe, Jr., and Jonathan Ward McPherson;
and in memory of Merrill W. Bowen, Jr.

CONTENTS

☒ *Note on Photos* ☒

Many of the illustrations and photographs used in this book are old, historical images. The quality of the prints is not always up to current standards because in many cases the originals are from old or poor quality negatives or the originals are damaged. The content of the illustrations, however, made their inclusion important despite problems in reproduction.

AUTHORS' NOTE

At least 800 unique tribes, or bands, of Indian people lived in the Americas at the time Europeans first arrived there in 1492. A tribe is a community or group of families who share the same culture, or way of living. The things that make up a culture can range from clothing and housing styles to ways of singing or praying. They include how people make and decorate the objects that they use in their daily lives. Tribal members speak the same language. Sometimes the language they speak is similar to the one that their neighbors speak. It could also be very different. A list of tribes of Indian people is located at the end of this book.

American Indians were and continue to be skilled at adapting to the places where they live. From the start, the features of the land where Indian people lived and the plants and animals that they found there influenced their way of life. Their cultures were also shaped by the climate and by neighboring tribes. Tribes that lived in similar regions developed many of the same ways of doing things. For example, they used many of the same medicines and developed similar styles of art. The geographical regions where similar tribes live are called culture areas. The list of tribes at the end of the book is divided into culture areas. Maps of these culture areas are also located at the back of this book. The maps contain the names of tribes that live in these areas.

Over time tribes and their cultures change. Some of the tribes mentioned in this book existed hundreds or thousands of years ago, but they do not exist as groups today. The people themselves did not vanish. Their language changed along with their way of doing things. Sometimes they moved. Sometimes they became part of other tribes.

When non-Indians saw the earth mounds that Indian people had built at Cahokia, near what is now St. Louis, Missouri, they refused to believe that Indian people made them. Instead they thought that the mounds must have been built by people who were not related to the Indians living at the time the Europeans had arrived in the Americas.

As non-Indians took more and more land for themselves, they displaced more and more American Indians. In Mesoamerica and South America, the Indian cities became Spanish cities. Indian people were forced to work for the Europeans and live the way they dictated. In North America, the U.S. and Canadian governments moved Indian people from the land where they lived to reservations or reserves. Indian people were discouraged from living in houses of their own design and from wearing their traditional clothing. Because so much of their art reflected their spiritual beliefs and kept their history alive, they were discouraged from creating art as well. Often Indian people were punished for trying to keep their traditional way of life.

In the meantime, American schoolchildren were taught that Indians were ignorant and that their way of living was inferior. This went on for many years. *Halleck's History of Our Country,* a popular elementary school textbook in 1923, told children, ". . . the Indian was ignorant, and no great teacher had come to him. He had few tools, and most of these were of wood or stone. We could scarcely build a hen coop to-day with such tools." Generations of people believed this and other untruths.

Since that time archaeologists started to rediscover the truth about how American Indians had lived before 1492. They now know for certain that the ancestors of the American Indians alive today built the cities that so impressed the conquistadores. They understand that, rather than trying to change the world around them to suit their needs, American Indians adapted to the world where they found themselves living. With efficient tools, they built comfortable houses and made practical clothing.

Today modern environmental scientists are concerned about how much timber Americans use to build their homes. These scientists also worry about how many energy resources are used to heat and cool modern homes and power modern cities. As they search for solutions to these problems, many look to the traditional lifestyles of Native peoples for answers about how to live in harmony with the environment.

Houses of Snow and Houses of Wood

Indians throughout the Americas built homes in a number of styles. The design of their homes depended on the climate where they lived and the materials that they used to make these dwellings. For example, the Inuit of the Arctic region created their winter homes from snow and ice, two building materials that were in abundant supply where they lived. Indians of the North American Northwest lived surrounded by large cedar trees. They cut these trees into planks and used the lumber to build wooden houses with siding and pitched (sloped) roofs. Like the Indians of the Northwest, American Indians living in the Amazon Basin used wood for their homes. Because the climate where they lived was very warm, they did not build exterior walls of wood. Instead they often built homes without walls in order to allow airflow to cool them.

IGLOOS OF THE ARCTIC

The Inuit people of the Arctic built two types of dome-shaped houses of compacted snow. Inuit people who lived near the ocean made small snow houses for temporary shelters when they hunted. One person could build a small house in an hour or two. The Inuit people who lived in the interior polar regions built larger snow houses. They lived in these circular dwellings throughout the winter. Their igloos were from six to 15 feet in diameter and about six feet high. They housed five or six people. Usually it took two people to build a large snow home.

Before Inuit igloo builders began making a snow home, they probed snowdrifts with a wooden rod to find the right kind of snow

The Inuit called their snow homes iglu. Later English speakers spelled this word *igloo*.

for building. The best snow was compact and was not layered. When they found good snow, one member of the two-person team cut the blocks from the snow with a bone knife made especially for this purpose. The size of the blocks that they cut depended on the firmness of the snow and the size of the igloo. Bigger igloos required bigger blocks. The remaining builder fitted the snow blocks together to form a foundation. Then the builder laid more blocks on top of this base in a spiral. For the most part, igloo builders were men.

After the builder had finished the foundation, the snow cutter carved blocks from the inside of this circle. The other builder stood outside the circle, arranging the blocks so that they leaned toward the interior. In this way the building team made a vault or dome. The cutter made the blocks larger than necessary so that the builder could trim the excess in order to make sure that the spiral was even and the blocks fit together exactly. Once the snow block had been

Trees were scarce in the Arctic, but snow was in plentiful supply. The Inuit used this natural resource to make their winter homes. *(National Archives of Canada/Photograph No. PA-055575)*

placed, the builder hammered it. This not only gave it a solid fit; the hammering caused the snow to start to melt. It quickly refroze, sealing the block into place.

Finally, when there was room left for only one block at the top, the Inuit cut an ice block to cap the top. From the inside of the house they twisted it securely into place. Because the rows of blocks were tilted inward, their weight pushed against the block in the center of the roof. It kept the other blocks from collapsing and made the igloo very sturdy.

At this point women and children often helped by chinking, or filling, the cracks between the blocks with loose snow to keep out the wind.

A small igloo that was used as a temporary shelter by hunters could be built by one person in about two hours. *(Canadian Geological Survey/Library of Congress, Prints and Photographs Division [LC-USZ62-103522])*

They also covered the outside of the igloo with a layer of snow and smoothed it with flat snow shovels. Since snow served as insulation, keeping the heat inside, igloos were remarkably warm inside even in the coldest weather.

Igloo builders cut a window from freshwater ice and put that in place. Fresh water froze more readily and froze clearer than seawater. They also made a vent hole so that smoke from whale oil lamps could escape. They built one or two smaller domes and attached them to the main igloo with snow block tunnels to serve as an entry-way. This prevented cold air from entering the home when people came and went. Sometimes they added a windbreak made from snow blocks outside the entry-way door to further prevent drafts from entering their homes. They made small domes attached to the living area to serve as storage closets for clothing and hunting equipment. Other domes sheltered sled dogs from the cold. Small domes also served as cold storage for surplus meat.

A MATTER OF LIFE AND DEATH

Arctic temperatures remain well below freezing for nine months of the year. Because of the angle of the Sun to the Earth, these months have very long nights and short days. In the winter Arctic temperatures average from −35 to −50 degrees Fahrenheit. It is not unusual for the temperature to dip much lower. The cold, combined with strong winds that are common in the Arctic, makes keeping warm a matter of life and death.

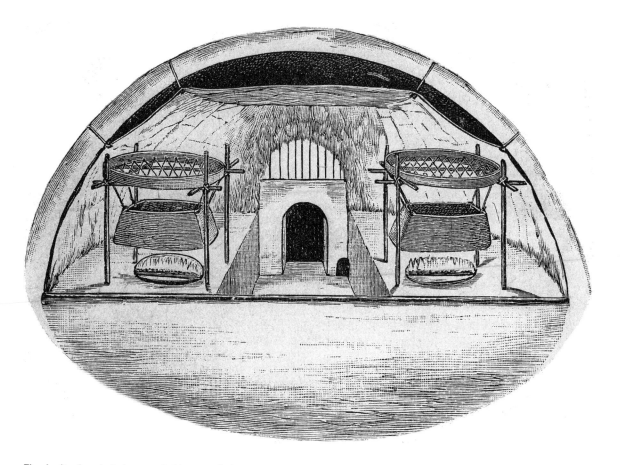

The Inuit placed their wet clothing on drying racks inside their igloos. They also used wide containers to hold snow that they melted to provide themselves with drinking water. *(Library of Congress, Prints and Photographs Division ([LC-USZ62-132784])*

Sometimes four or five Inuit families who were related or were very good friends built their igloos close together and connected them with snow tunnels to a much larger domed snow house. This central igloo served as a community room where people danced, told stories, feasted, and played games together without having to go outside.

The first Europeans to see igloos were amazed at how cozy they were inside. The Inuit lined the walls with sealskin that helped keep cold air out and kept the oil lamps that they used as heaters from melting the snow walls. In some areas of the Arctic these lamps were carved from soapstone. The polar Inuit soaked moss in fat and then lit it with dry moss tinder. They set it afire by striking an iron pyrite stone against a quartz stone to make a spark. When the moss burned, they set it on a walrus shoulder blade that contained blubber, which served as fuel.

Inuit people furnished their igloos with large sleeping platforms made of snow. They covered them with baleen (the bony plates from whales' mouths) or willow mats that were topped with hides. Platforms woven from sinew held damp clothing, so it could dry above more lamps. Sinew is the tough tissue that holds animals' muscles to their bones. The Inuit also hung sealskins full of snow above their lamps. When it melted, they used it for drinking water.

If an igloo began to melt in the winter, builders could make a new, slightly larger, snow house over the outside of the old one. When they had completed the new home, they took apart the blocks of the old one and carried them out through the entryway door. In springtime when it melted, they did not bother to rebuild. Leaving the lower walls in place, they stretched hides over the roof in order to stay warm and dry.

Even though the Arctic is bitterly cold in the winter, in the summer the temperature rises to 50 degrees Fahrenheit. In some places it is even warmer. Days grow longer until the summer solstice, when there is no darkness at night. The Inuit built tents that they called *tupiks* each summer when they could no longer live in their igloos. Coastal Inuit used whale rib bones to make a domed frame that they covered with sealskins. Inuit who lived further inland used wooden poles and covered them with caribou hides. They insulated these summer houses with dried moss.

▲▼▲▼▲▼▲▼▲▼▲▼▲▼▲▼▲▼▲▼▲▼▲▼▲

AN INUIT INVENTION
Many of the first non-Indians to study the Inuit did not believe that Indians could have engineered the vaulted roofs of their domed houses. They thought instead that Europeans had taught the Inuit to make igloos. This theory did not agree with Inuit oral history or the records of the earliest European explorers. Eventually these researchers admitted that the Inuit had invented this unique style of building on their own.

▼▲▼▲▼▲▼▲▼▲▼▲▼▲▼▲▼▲▼▲▼▲▼▲▼

PLANK HOUSES OF THE NORTHWEST AND CALIFORNIA

The temperate rain forest is a ribbon of land stretching along the southernmost coast of what is now Alaska to Oregon. It is filled with

> Cedar is so useful that it is one of the most popular woods used by builders in the United States for siding and shingles today.

many varieties of spruce trees, balsam firs, and western red cedar trees. Ocean currents and winds keep the climate of the Northwest mild, but the winters are cool. Parts of the Northwest rain forest receive more than 80 inches of rainfall a year. Keeping dry was one of the main concerns of Indians who lived in the Northwest.

They used western red cedar wood when they built their homes. Red cedar is an evergreen tree that contains thujic acid, a natural resin. This sticky substance makes it water resistant. Cedar wood resists warping in wet weather. The resin in red cedar also repels insects and rodents. In addition, it is a good insulator, preventing cool air from seeping into homes and warm interior air from leaking outside.

Haida builders made their homes from cedar, a wood that is still used by builders today. This picture was taken in British Columbia, Canada, in 1878 at Skedans Village. (*Geological Survey of Canada Collection/National Archives of Canada/Photograph No. PA-38148*)

American Indians of the northwest Pacific Coast did not have to move in search of food as many other hunters and gatherers did. The streams where they lived were filled with salmon, and the sea contained abundant herring, seals, and whales. The forest provided many edible plants. Indians of the Northwest could remain in permanent villages and build plank-covered post-and-beam houses to live in.

▲▼▲▼▲▼▲▼▲▼▲▼▲▼▲▼▲▼▲▼▲▼▲▼▲

CARPENTRY TOOLS

Builders of Northwest tribes invented a number of specialized woodworking tools made of bone, stone, horn, and wood. When British navy captain James Cook sailed into Nootka Sound on Vancouver Island, he was the first European that the Nootka people had seen. His men examined a Nootka carpenter's toolbox and found a maul, chisels, wedges, adzes, simple drills, sandstone grindstones, and sharkskin that served as fine sandpaper. More recently, archaeologists have found beaver tooth and mussel shell knives as well as stone drills at the Ozette site located on the tip of what is now the Olympic Peninsula, west of Seattle. Early Makah carpenters made these tools, which have been dated to A.D. 800.

▼▲▼▲▼▲▼▲▼▲▼▲▼▲▼▲▼▲▼▲▼▲▼▲▼

Plank homes varied in size. The smaller ones were from 14 to 20 feet wide and 20 to 60 feet long. The Dwamish of what is now Washington State built homes that were 60 feet wide and hundreds of feet long. These huge homes contained separate spaces for many families in addition to a large common room. Besides a large, shared central fire in the common room, each family space had its own cooking fire.

The first step in building a post-and-beam home was harvesting the wood. Indian carpenters cut long poles to form the frame for their home. Then they cut planks, or boards, for the home's walls. Many trees of the temperate rain forest grow to huge sizes. American Indian builders felled these big trees by making a large hole in the side of the tree and setting a slow fire in it. Eventually the fire would burn through the trunk and the tree would fall. Next they split the trunk into planks by driving wooden wedges into it.

The Haida, who lived in what are now the northern Queen Charlotte Islands, off the western coast of Canada, perfected the art of plank-home building. They were masters of mortise-and-tenon joining. A mortise is a hole drilled into a piece of wood. A tenon is a projection that has been carved on another piece of wood. Putting two wooden beams together by fitting a tenon into a mortise is one of the strongest bonds for joining wood.

The inside of this Chinook lodge from the Northwest Coast was drawn in 1844. A sunken fire pit held a fire that was used to heat the lodge and for cooking meals. *(Richard W. Dodson, Engraver/Library of Congress, Prints and Photographs Division [LC-USZ62-98769])*

Often the Haida shaped the wooden planks they used for siding by steaming and bending them so that they would overlap and produce weathertight walls. They covered the gabled, or peaked, roofs of their homes with larger planks fastened so that they could be moved. These skylights let in fresh air and light or let out smoke, and they could be closed when it rained. On windy days, the residents placed stones on the roofs to hold the planks in place.

Other tribes of the Northwest also built houses with peaked roofs. Some builders of the Northwest, including the Dwamish and other Salish-speaking tribes, made houses with slanted roofs. These roofs were highest at the front of the house and sloped to the back to allow rainwater to run off them. Builders carved grooves into the roof planks so that they would lock together when they were overlapped. Many Indians of the Northwest insulated their homes from the inside with cedar bark.

American Indians of what is now Northern California also built plank houses from cedar wood or redwood. Like cedar, redwood repels insects and does not easily rot. Both the Yuroks and the Hupa dug pits in the ground so that the walls of their pitched-roof houses were partially underground. They used notches in the wood to fit the frame of their homes together.

POLE HOUSES OF THE SOUTHEAST, CIRCUM-CARIBBEAN, AND AMAZON BASIN

American Indians of the southernmost part of what are now Florida, the Caribbean Islands, and parts of the Amazon Basin lived in an extremely warm and wet climate. During the warmest months of the year, temperatures average about 90 degrees Fahrenheit in these places. The air often contains 80 to 90 percent humidity. Because perspiration, the body's natural cooling system, does not evaporate well at high humidity, the air often feels even warmer than the thermometer indicates. In order to remain comfortable, American Indians of these regions built open houses framed with wooden poles and topped with thatched roofs.

In what is now southern Florida, the Seminole and Miccosukee people called these dwellings chickees. *Chickee* is the Seminole word for home. Chickee builders began by sinking four sturdy cypress wood poles into the ground to form the corners of a house. Then they lashed more poles to the top to make a frame for a pitched roof. They covered this frame with several layers of palmetto leaves so that the rain would not drip into the

CAMOUFLAGE HOUSES

The Seminole were originally southern Creek and lived in what are now Georgia and Alabama. There they lived in log houses. In the 1700s they moved south to what is now Florida. Because the Seminole hid runaway slaves, General Andrew Jackson led the U.S. Army against them in the First Seminole War. When he became U.S. president, he tried to force them to move to Indian Territory in what is now Oklahoma. Many Seminole people escaped to the south, hid in the everglades and began fighting the U.S. Army. The Seminole began living in chickees because they were quick to build. This allowed them to keep moving their camps. Chickees also blended so well with the swampy landscape that army troops could not see them from a distance.

shelter. (The palmetto is a type of palm tree that grows more than 50 feet high. Its fan-shaped leaves can be from three to nine feet long.) Chickee builders laid crossed poles on top of the roof to secure the thatching.

Chickee builders completed their homes by lashing, or tying, a platform to the corner poles of the house. This floor, which was raised about three feet from the ground, allowed breezes to circulate beneath the house. It also served as protection from snakes, alligators, and insects. The Seminole slept on the platforms at night. During the day, they sat on the platforms to work. When the weather was hot, they put water on the sides of their chickee. When the water evaporated, it cooled the air inside the house. The Seminole cooked in a separate chickee that did not have a platform so that they could build a fire directly on the earth.

Open-sided pole buildings that resembled chickees except for the raised platform were common throughout the Circum-Caribbean and the Amazon Basin. Most Indian people in the region used open-sided pole buildings as places to cook. Sometimes they built thatched roofs that extended almost to the ground on the buildings where they slept. Builders sometimes covered the walls of buildings where they slept or stored possessions with palmetto leaf thatching.

People of the tropical rain forest of the Amazon Basin in South America used wood from cashew trees for poles when they built their homes. Like red cedar of the Northwest, cashew wood is resistant to damaging insects. Amazon builders joined wooden poles together by lashing them with vines. When the vines dried, they created a stronger bond that lasted up to 20 years even in the humid, tropical climate. Sometimes Indians of the Amazon Basin used mahogany as a building material for their homes. This hard tropical wood is strong, waterproof, and resists rotting. Mahogany also contains a natural insect repellent.

Although most of these homes did not have sleeping platforms that allowed air to circulate, American Indians invented a cool and comfort-

In warm climates, Indian cooks prepared meals in a separate building that served as a kitchen. This kept their sleeping quarters as cool as possible. These women of the Circum-Caribbean are making tortillas.
(Newberry Library/Stock Montage)

A Carib Indian sits outside his house in this picture made in 1900 in Nicaragua. The sturdy wooden frames of pole homes kept them standing during tropical storms. Indian builders used wood that resisted moisture and insects. (*Library of Congress, Prints and Photographs Division [LC-USZ62-98087]*)

able way to sleep. They wove nets from cotton and other fibers. They tied the ends of these nets, now known as hammocks, to the poles of their homes. Christopher Columbus was so impressed with hammocks that he mentioned them in his journal.

2

Houses of Fiber and Bark and Houses of Hide

 American Indians of the Northeast and eastern subarctic regions of North America framed their houses with saplings or poles. They covered these frames with mats made from cattails or with sheets of bark. These one- or two-family homes were called wigwams. Most of them were dome-shaped, but some of them were cone-shaped. The Iroquois and Huron of the Northeast built longhouses in much the same way. Longhouses were often very large, housing many families in one dwelling. Indians of the northern Great Plains and western Plateau made cone-shaped tipis. They covered these portable houses with hides, or animal skins.

WIGWAMS OF THE NORTHEAST

American Indian builders made the frames for their wigwams from saplings, young trees that could be easily bent. To make a wigwam, men cut the trees that would serve as the frame. The Anishinabe (Chippewa or Ojibway) used elm, hickory, willow, birch, or basswood saplings for wigwam frames. When they had cut the trees and stripped the bark from them, they drew a circle on the ground. This circle formed the floor plan for the wigwam. Most wigwams were about 14 feet in diameter and five to eight feet high.

The men, who framed wigwams, dug evenly spaced holes around the circle and set saplings into the holes, packing down the

▲▽▲▽▲▽▲▽▲▽▲▽▲▽▲▽▲▽▲▽▲▽▲▽▲▽▲▽▲

WHAT *WIGWAM* MEANS

Wigwam, or *wikwam,* is an Algonquian word that means "their dwelling," or "home." It comes from the root word *wik* that means "to dwell," or "to live in a place." The word *wickiup* also comes from this same source. A wickiup is a temporary shelter made of brush and branches that are lashed together to form a hut. Wickiups may have a very simple frame or no frame at all. Tribes of the Great Basin lived in wickiups in the summer. Some bands of Apache of the Southwest lived in wickiups that were thatched with yucca. Indians of the Great Basin and the Apache of the Southwest do not speak Algonquian languages. Europeans applied the Algonquian word to their homes.

▼▲▼▲▼▲▼▲▼▲▼▲▼▲▼▲▼▲▼▲▼▲▼▲▼▲▼▲▼

earth to make sure that they would stay in place. They tied the saplings together at the top with split oak roots or the inner layer of basswood bark. This formed a dome. To make the frame even sturdier they bent saplings and wove them around it. The builders lashed these hoops to the upright poles with more roots or bark. They finished the wigwam frame by lashing the saplings together at every place they crossed.

After the wigwam frame had been completed, the women covered it with large mats that they had sewn from cattail stalks. The mats were from four to six feet wide and from eight to 10 feet long. To make the mats, the women tied a cord made from fiber between two stakes or trees. Then they separated the cattails into bundles that contained four leaves. They placed the ends of these bundles on the taut string that they had stretched across the space between the trees. They folded the ends of the leaves over it and wove another string back and forth to hold them in place. After this they began sewing

▲▽▲▽▲▽▲▽▲▽▲▽▲▽▲▽▲▽▲▽▲▽▲▽▲▽▲▽▲

A PRACTICAL DESIGN

Dome-shaped wigwams did not offer much resistance to the wind. The air flowed around these homes rather than pushing directly against them. Because of this, they remained standing even in strong storms.

▼▲▼▲▼▲▼▲▼▲▼▲▼▲▼▲▼▲▼▲▼▲▼▲▼▲▼▲▼

▲▼▲▼▲▼▲▼▲▼▲▼▲▼▲▼▲▼▲▼▲▼▲▼▲▼▲

NEEDLES AND CORD

Mat makers of the Northeast sewed the cattails or rushes together with long needles made from bone. The rib bones of deer made the best needles. They used spruce roots, milkweed, nettle, or hemp fibers for cord.

▼▲▼▲▼▲▼▲▼▲▼▲▼▲▼▲▼▲▼▲▼▲▼▲▼▲▼

through each bundle of cattails. The mat makers were careful to overlap each bundle of stalks so that after they tied them onto the wigwam frame, no rain would leak inside. Once the women had sewn all the way across the mat, they began another row of stitching four to six inches farther down. Once they had finished the mats, they tied them in overlapping rows to the frame.

Indian women of the Northeast also made mats for the inside of their wigwams. These mats provided extra insurance against leaks and also helped to keep the wigwam warm on cool nights. The air trapped between the two layers of mats was a good insulator. (This

Women from the Consolidated Chippewa Agency in Minnesota sit in front of a dome-shaped wigwam. It is covered with sheets of birch bark. On the right it is covered with a woven mat of rushes or cattails. This picture was taken in 1915. *(National Archives and Records Administration Central Plains Region/Photograph No. NRE-75-COCH[PHO]-623)*

is why many windows today are double paned.) Besides keeping the wigwam snug, these mats served as a decoration.

Instead of sewing the inside mats, Indian women wove them. They used rushes, which are finer than cattails. With their fingers, they wove twisted fiber back and forth across the slats. When they had finished weaving the mats, they painted designs on them with plant dyes or embroidered them with fiber. When they moved, Indian people of the Northeast kept the mats that the women had woven. Rolling them up, they carried them to their new homes.

Inside their wigwams, Indians made sleeping platforms along the walls from pieces of wood. They tied the beds to the frame of the wigwam, one to two feet from the ground. To make these platforms softer, Indian women covered them with sleeping mats that they had braided from rushes. Then they covered these mats with hides.

Wigwam builders scooped earth from the dirt floor to make a shallow hole in the center of the house. This was where they built the fire to cook and keep themselves warm. The smoke from this fire rose through an opening they left at the top of the wigwam. To keep the wigwam covering from catching fire, Indians of the Northeast covered the edges of the mats that they had placed around the smoke hole with mud. Baked hard by the heat, the mud served as fireproofing.

Winters in the Northeast are cold and often windy, so in the wintertime Indians covered their wigwams with sheets of bark instead of mats. Sometimes they used a combination of the two. They sewed sections of bark together into long rolls. Because bark is stiff when it dries, they heated the rolls over a fire so that they would more easily bend. Sometimes Indians of the Northeast stuffed the space between the bark and the inside mats with plant fiber such as milkweed or cattail fluff for

▲▽▲▽▲▽▲▽▲▽▲▽▲▽▲▽▲▽▲▽▲▽▲▽▲▽▲

HOUSES OF GRASS

The Caddo and Wichita of the Plains made houses that were taller but otherwise similar in shape to the wigwams of the Northeast. Men used willow saplings to make the frame. Women gathered tall grass and tied it in bundles, and then they sewed the bundles of grass to the frames with long needles that they made from cottonwood. Some tribes of the Southeast and what is now California made somewhat similar domed houses of grass.

▼▲▼▲▼▲▼▲▼▲▼▲▼▲▼▲▼▲▼▲▼▲▼▲▼▲▼▲▼

even more insulation. They covered the door with a hide to make sure that the warm air stayed inside.

Some Indians of the Northeast and the eastern subarctic built wigwams that were cone shaped. Instead of bending saplings and tying them together at the top in order to make a frame, they used straight poles that were about five feet long. These wigwam builders set the poles into a circle and leaned them against each other at the top. Then they tied them at the top and covered them with sheets of bark. Archaeologists believe they began building this style of wigwam about 5,000 years ago. Some tribes of California and Great Basin Indians also built and lived in cone-shaped structures covered with bark.

Many of the wigwams made by American Indians who lived near the Great Lakes were cone-shaped. The woman standing in front of this one is stirring maple syrup beneath an arbor. In the summer Indian people covered arbors with evergreen boughs to provide shade. This photo was taken at the Red Lake Indian Agency in Minnesota in 1939. *(National Archives and Records Administration Central Plains Region/Photograph No. NRE-75-RL[PHO]-1072)*

This picture of a Chippewa, or Anishinabe, camp was taken in Canada between 1872 and 1875. *(National Archives of Canada/Photograph No. C-004092)*

LONGHOUSES OF THE NORTHEAST

The Iroquois and Huron, who lived in the Northeast, had been building longhouses long before Europeans arrived. These large buildings were usually about 20 feet high and 20 feet wide. They varied in length from 30 feet to several hundred feet. Some of the early longhouses that they built were huge—longer than a football field.

Longhouses needed to be quite large because they housed extended families that included grandparents, aunts, uncles, and cousins. As more people married into a family, the residents of a longhouse added onto one end of it in order to make room for the newcomers. When men married, they lived in the longhouses that belonged to the wife's family.

Like wigwam makers, longhouse builders began constructing their homes by making a wooden frame. They cut poles from areas where fires had killed the larger old trees or from land that they had cleared for fields and then had later abandoned. These new trees, called second growth, made good posts because they were straight

Longhouses held several families. The original caption on this picture, which was drawn in the late 1500s, says: "The towne of Pomeiock and true forme of their houses, covered and enclosed some w[i]th matts and some w[i]th barks of trees. All compassed about w[i]th smale poles stock thick together in stedd of a wall." The mats could be removed in the summer in order to allow the air to circulate. *(Library of Congress, Prints and Photographs Division [LC-USZ62-582])*

and thin. After the builders had trimmed their poles to the right length, they removed all of the bark from them. This step kept insects from making their homes in the longhouse frame. It also provided Indian builders of the Northeast with bark, which was another important building material.

When the builders finished preparing the poles for a longhouse, they measured a large rectangle on the ground. Next they dug holes in the earth and set the posts around the perimeter of what would become the longhouse. They also set two rows of posts down the center of the longhouse to make a center hallway or aisle. Once they had sunk the posts firmly into the ground, they tied more poles across them in order to make the longhouse frame strong.

▲▼▲▼▲▼▲▼▲▼▲▼▲▼▲▼▲▼▲▼▲▼▲▼▲

BARK FASTENERS

American Indian builders made both large and small houses with no nails. Instead, they wrapped plant fiber around wood to hold poles together. Some of the plant stalks that builders of the Northeast used were dogbane, or Indian hemp, and milkweed, as well as cattail. To make cord from these materials, American Indians pounded the plants to separate the fibers. Then they soaked them in water to soften the fibers. Finally they twisted together two strands of fiber. Indians used much the same process to make cord from bark and roots. Bark and roots were tougher, so they had to be soaked in water and wood ash before the fibers could be separated.

▼▲▼▲▼▲▼▲▼▲▼▲▼▲▼▲▼▲▼▲▼▲▼▲▼

They shaped the roof into a bow by bending green saplings into an arch and lashing them to the upright poles that made up the long walls of the frame. Then they lashed straight poles along the length of the longhouse roof to make it sturdier. The half-circle, or semicircle, shape of longhouse roofs allowed rain to run off them easily and prevented snow from building up and caving in the roofs.

When they had finished the frame, the builders covered the walls and the roof of a longhouse with sheets of bark. Indian builders harvested bark in the springtime when it was easiest to peel from tree trunks. The Iroquois liked to use elm bark because they could peel it from the trees in large sheets. They also used walnut bark. After they had gathered enough bark for the coming year's building projects, they lay it on the ground and placed rocks on it so that it would dry flat. Elm bark was very strong when it dried—almost as strong as the plywood that builders use today. Some tribes of the Northeast tied mats to the outer longhouse walls instead of bark. They rolled up the mats in the summer to keep the longhouse cool.

The Iroquois and Huron made two doors in their longhouses, one at each end. They used hides or sewn mats to cover the doors. They often built a flat roof over the door, much like a porch, that helped to keep the rain and snow out. Although the ends of some longhouses were straight, most were rounded. Families used these rounded ends for storage. Longhouse builders insulated their homes

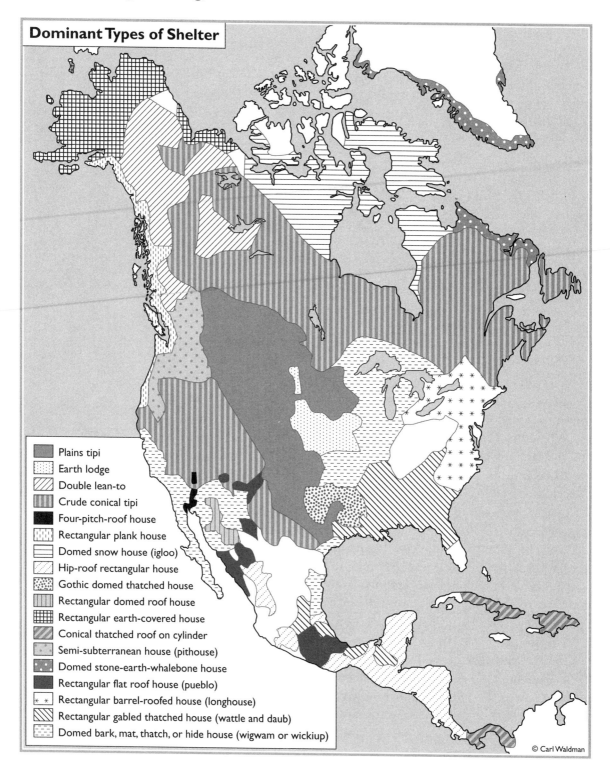

Dominant Types of Shelter

- Plains tipi
- Earth lodge
- Double lean-to
- Crude conical tipi
- Four-pitch-roof house
- Rectangular plank house
- Domed snow house (igloo)
- Hip-roof rectangular house
- Gothic domed thatched house
- Rectangular domed roof house
- Rectangular earth-covered house
- Conical thatched roof on cylinder
- Semi-subterranean house (pithouse)
- Domed stone-earth-whalebone house
- Rectangular flat roof house (pueblo)
- Rectangular barrel-roofed house (longhouse)
- Rectangular gabled thatched house (wattle and daub)
- Domed bark, mat, thatch, or hide house (wigwam or wickiup)

© Carl Waldman

▲▼▲▼▲▼▲▼▲▼▲▼▲▼▲▼▲▼▲▼▲▼▲▼▲▼▲

QUONSET HUTS

Quonset huts are lightweight, portable buildings that are easily and quickly constructed. They are made up of a skeleton of semicircular ribs covered by corrugated steel. These buildings were invented at the beginning of World War II to inexpensively house military personnel. The builders of these Quonset huts reinvented the time-tested design of Huron and Iroquois longhouses.

▼▲▼▲▼▲▼▲▼▲▼▲▼▲▼▲▼▲▼▲▼▲▼▲▼▲▼

from the inside with fur hides or woven mats that they hung on the walls.

On the inside the longhouses were divided into apartments that were about 20 feet long. One family, consisting of parents and their children, lived in each apartment space. The two families that lived across from each other shared a cooking fire in the aisle between their apartments. Beds and storage space lined the walls. The Iroquois built beds that were like benches. These were about a foot from the ground. They covered their sleeping platforms with bark sheets and on top of that they placed hides and furs. Above their beds, longhouse residents built another platform.

Arthur C. Parker, an Iroquois of the Seneca tribe, writing in the early 20th century, said that these bunks were similar in appearance to upper and lower beds in a train's sleeping car. Indian people slept in lower bunks in winter so that they would be near the fire. Most of the time they used the top bed for storing personal items, but occasionally they used it for sleeping as well.

TIPIS OF THE GREAT PLAINS AND PLATEAU

Tipi is the Lakota, Dakota, Nakota word for home. (These people were historically called the Sioux.) The tipis that the Indians of the Plains and Plateau region lived in were cone-shaped like some of the wigwams that Indians of the Northeast built. Many of the tribes that lived in tipis once lived in the Northeast. Archaeologists, scientists who study the past, believe that these Indians once lived in cone-shaped wigwams.

▲▽▲▽▲▽▲▽▲▽▲▽▲▽▲▽▲▽▲▽▲▽▲▽▲▽▲▽▲

TALL AND BEAUTIFUL DWELLINGS
Spanish explorer Francisco Vásquez de Coronado first saw tipis sometime between 1540 and 1542. They were the dwellings of a group of buffalo-hunting American Indians who wintered with the Pueblo people. Coronado wrote that the tents were tall and beautiful.

▽▲▽▲▽▲▽▲▽▲▽▲▽▲▽▲▽▲▽▲▽▲▽▲▽▲▽▲▽

Trees are scarce on the plains and in many places so are rushes and reeds. Plains Indians often had to travel long distances to find trees suitable for making poles. It would have taken too much time away from hunting for them to travel far enough to find bark and reeds. Because Indians of the plains were hunters and gatherers, they moved often. That meant that they needed to find a way to build homes that were easy to take down, move, and set up again. Tipis were a good solution to these challenges.

Because buffalo were plentiful on the plains, Indians covered their tipis with the hide from these animals. They adapted the design of their homes to their environment in other ways as well. Since the Great Plains are flat and treeless, nothing stops or slows the wind as it blows. Often the wind gusts from 50 to 80 miles an hour. Tipis were aerodynamic—their slanted sides allowed strong prairie winds to pass around them. Tipi builders changed the floor plan of their dwellings to an oval to make the tipis less likely to tip over. They also tilted the pole frame by using longer poles on one side to give them even more stability. Since they sewed the hide covering into one piece, the wind could not catch parts of it and rip it from the frame.

Although Indian men cut the tipi poles, the

▲▽▲▽▲▽▲▽▲▽▲▽▲▽▲▽▲▽▲▽▲▽▲▽▲▽▲▽▲

EARLY TIPIS
Before the Spaniards introduced horses to the plains, Indians used dogs to pull tipi poles and covers when they moved camp. This meant that tipis had to be relatively small. Juan de Oñate, a Spanish explorer who traveled from what is now New Mexico to the southwestern plains in 1599, described seeing early tipis made of tanned hides that were "very bright red and white in color and bell-shaped, with flaps and openings and built skillfully as any house in Italy." According to Oñate the tipis did not weigh more than 50 pounds.

▽▲▽▲▽▲▽▲▽▲▽▲▽▲▽▲▽▲▽▲▽▲▽▲▽▲▽▲▽

women made the covers. The women owned the tipis, or lodges, as they were sometimes called. The women were responsible for setting them up and taking them down. Two women could erect a tipi in an hour or two. They began by laying three or four tall foundation poles together on the ground and lashing them together, a few feet from the top. Next they set this tripod upright. After they had pulled each of the tripod's legs apart, they leaned more poles into the spaces at the top of the tripod.

Before they set up a tipi, women spent many months tanning buffalo hides for the covers. Once they had tanned the hides, they pieced them together and sewed tight seams with bone needles and buffalo sinew. When they had finished the sewing, they cut a cover into a semicircle shape. To put the cover onto the tipi, they tied the middle of the flat edge to a lifting pole and raised it into position at the back of the tipi. Next they pulled the corners of the semicircle toward the door. After they had smoothed the cover over the tipi frame, they held it together with long wooden pegs. Finally, the women placed stones around the edges of the covering to keep it in place. Today archaeologists study these circular arrangements of stones, called tipi rings, to learn more about where Plains Indians traveled and hunted.

Tipis were very comfortable places to live. The smoke hole at the top could be opened and closed by adjusting poles that were tied to flaps that were part of the covering. This design drew air in from the doorway and from beneath the tipi cover. Then the air was pulled back outside through the smoke hole. The airflow carried the smoke with it. This was important during the cold winters, when Indians spent most of their time inside their tipis.

▲▼▲▼▲▼▲▼▲▼▲▼▲▼▲▼▲▼▲▼▲▼▲▼▲▼▲▼▲

TIPIS OF THE PLATEAU

The Nez Perce of the Plateau Region also lived in tipis of similar design. Before the horse was introduced to them, they did not hunt as much as Plains Indians did. Instead of using hides to cover their tipis, they used mats that they had sewn. After they began hunting buffalo on horseback, they began covering their tipis with hides.

▼▲▼▲▼▲▼▲▼▲▼▲▼▲▼▲▼▲▼▲▼▲▼▲▼▲▼▲▼

Tipis could be put up and taken down within hours, so that entire villages could easily be moved. When non-Indian hunters made the buffalo nearly extinct, Indian people began covering tipis with canvas rather than buffalo hides. *(Library of Congress, Prints and Photographs Division [LC-USZ62-55635])*

When the weather was bitterly cold, Indians banked snow around their tipis to keep warm air from escaping. Northern plains tribes used hide liners for their tipis in the wintertime in order to create dead air space that served as insulation. Often they painted these liners with bright designs. Sometimes they used double liners and stuffed grass between the layers of hide. They made tipi doors from hide. These doors could be fastened tightly to keep cold drafts from coming inside.

Tipi dwellers hung many of their belongings from the poles around the edges of the inside of the tipi. They stored smaller items, including food and medicine, in leather pouches and in boxes that they made from rawhide. They hung these from the tipi poles as well. Indians slept on the ground on buffalo robes, tanned hides with the fur left on them. They sat on the ground and leaned against backrests made of sticks.

Non-Indians recognized how practical and useful the tipis that American Indians had invented could be. Kit Carson, a white man who earned a

▲▼▲▼▲▼▲▼▲▼▲▼▲▼▲▼▲▼▲▼▲▼▲▼▲

CANVAS TIPIS

Once horses became part of their way of life, Plains Indians began making tipis that were 15 to 20 feet across. The poles became longer too. These tipi covers required from 15 to 20 hides. Later, after European settlement destroyed the great buffalo herds that once roamed the North American continent, American Indians began using canvas tipi covers. Because canvas is not as heavy as hide, they were able to make tipis that were 20 to 30 feet in diameter. At first the U.S. government issued this canvas to the Indian people. Later they stopped the practice in an attempt to force them to live in permanent wooden or log houses on reservations.

▼▲▼▲▼▲▼▲▼▲▼▲▼▲▼▲▼▲▼▲▼▲▼▲▼

reputation as an Indian fighter, insisted that explorer and later politician John Charles Frémont pack a tipi when Carson accompanied him on his first expedition to what are now the Wind River Mountains in modern Wyoming. General H. H. Sibley of the U.S. Army was so impressed with the tipi design that he incorporated it into his design for the Sibley army tent, which was used by soldiers during the Plains Indian Wars of the 19th century.

3

Houses of Earth and Houses of Stone

The land that American Indians lived on provided them with soil and stones that could be used to make houses even when other building materials were scarce. Throughout the Americas, Indian builders used earth as a natural insulator to keep their homes warm in winter and cool in summer.

Some groups of Indian people built their homes into hillsides. Others made wooden framed houses with timbered or thatched roofs and mounded earth over them to provide protection from the weather. Yet other groups of Indians dug pits, or large holes, and then built houses over them that were partially underground.

Indian homebuilders of the desert Southwest, the Southeast, Mesoamerica, and South America were experts at building with mud. They created thick-walled homes from a special mixture of earth and water called adobe. Sometimes they used adobe by itself to build their houses. At other times they used it to plaster over walls that they built from rock. In many parts of the Americas, Indian builders used mud to cover houses that they had constructed from sticks and other plant materials.

Modern architects use some of the same methods that American Indians invented for building with earth in order to create energy-efficient housing. Today housing experts are taking another look at underground, or berm, housing as a low-cost way to build houses that are energy efficient.

EARTH LODGES OF THE PLAINS

Earth lodges are large homes that have earth banked around their walls and heaped on top of their roofs. The Mandan, Arikara, and

Hidatsa of the Northern Plains and the Pawnee of the Southern Plains built houses of this type. The soil protected the people who lived in earth lodges against the weather. Because these dwellings resembled hills, they served as camouflage and concealed the people who lived there from enemies.

The earth lodges of the Mandan, Arikara, and Hidatsa, who lived in what is now North Dakota, were round and were from 15 to 30 feet across. Indian people began building these structures in about A.D. 700 along streams that emptied into the Missouri River. To construct an earth lodge, builders began by sinking four huge central posts into the ground. Usually these posts were cottonwood logs from which they had stripped the bark. The builders joined these posts with crossbeams made from more logs that had been stripped. They used strong mortise-and-tenon joints to connect the logs to support the weight of the earth that would be heaped on the roof. Next they circled this basic frame with a wider ring of 12 posts and crossbeams. Finally they positioned rafters that radiated from the central support to the outer ring like the spokes of a wheel. These rafters supported the roof of the earth lodge.

When the builders had finished the basic frame, they covered it with slanting posts of split planks called puncheons. These puncheons supported the earthen walls and kept the soil from caving into the living area. Next the builders covered the house with slender poles and a layer of brush to hold in place the earth that they would next pile over the top of the house. The brush anchored the soil so that it would not erode, or wash away, in rainstorms.

▲▼▲▼▲▼▲▼▲▼▲▼▲▼▲▼▲▼▲▼▲▼▲▼▲▼▲

SODDIES

Early non-Indian settlers who homesteaded on the Great Plains starting in the mid-1800s also built sod houses, which were called soddies. The houses that they built from bricks of sod were square and had windows. The settlers borrowed some building techniques from the Indians. They used ridgepoles for the roof and covered them with brush. Then they covered this with sod. In 1894 a sod house with a wooden door cost less than four dollars to build.

▼▲▼▲▼▲▼▲▼▲▼▲▼▲▼▲▼▲▼▲▼▲▼▲▼▲▼

> Because wood was so scarce on the Plains, many homesteaders borrowed an idea from the Indians. They burned dried buffalo chips, or droppings, for heat and cooking.

Indians next covered the entire lodge with earth, leaving an open space at the top for a smoke hole and another opening for the doorway. The last thing they did to finish an earth lodge was to cover the top with sod, strips of grass still growing in earth. Within a short time, the earth lodge would look like a hill to someone standing in the distance.

The Indians of the Upper Missouri built a fire in the center of the earth lodge floor so that the people who lived there could cook and stay warm. Beside this fire stood a platform that they used for storing small amounts of food and for preparing it. They stored most of their food in underground food caches that they dug beneath the floor of the lodge.

Earth lodges, such as this one constructed by the Pawnee of the Great Plains, provided protection from the weather and served as an excellent defense against enemies. *(National Archives and Records Administration—College Park/Photograph No. NWDNS-106-INE-3)*

Indian earth lodge residents made a screen of wooden posts in front of the door to keep the wind out when someone opened the hide flap on the doorway. They covered the rafters with cattail roofing mats to keep dirt from falling into their homes. When it rained, these mats swelled so that they were watertight and kept out drafts. Earth lodge dwellers also covered the floor with layers of mats.

Old people and men of high honor slept closest to the fire in the earth lodge. Everyone else slept in beds that were arranged around the perimeter of the circle. Often these beds were made as platforms with tall posts, like a four-poster bed. The Indians spread three or four hides over the platform to make a compartment that was warm and private. People who lived in earth lodges made pillows from hides that they stuffed with antelope or buffalo fur.

The Pawnee, Omaha, Ponca, and Otoe, who lived in what are now Kansas and Nebraska, also built earth lodges. Their earliest earth lodges were rectangular. Later these tribes built circular structures that looked a great deal like those of the Indians living along the Upper Missouri River. Pawnee builders began their lodges by digging a large hole two to three feet deep so that the lodge would be partially underground. They used eight to 10 forked center posts for their lodges and laid crossbeams in the forks. Then they built the outer circle. The entrance of a Pawnee earth lodge was a long, downward-sloping tunnel. Pawnee builders framed this with poles as well. They made a swinging door for the lodge by stretching buffalo hide over a willow frame and making hinges from hide strips.

EARTH LODGES OF THE ARCTIC

The Inuit people who lived in what is now the McKenzie River region of Alaska built earth-covered lodges as well. These were shaped like a cross. The Inuit framed them with driftwood and covered them with earth and snow. Finally they poured water over this covering and let it freeze. The ice held the snow and earth in place. A long underground tunnel served as the entryway and blocked cold air from entering through the doorway. The Inuit builders made a skylight from a block of ice placed in the roof. Separate families lived in each of the wings of the home, which they occupied only part of the year. The rest of the time they lived in igloos.

The Inuit who lived in the west of what is now Greenland also built houses from sod and stones. They made windows that they framed with wood and covered with halibut stomachs or seal intestines to keep out the wind while letting in the light.

PIT HOUSES OF CALIFORNIA AND THE SOUTHWEST

In addition to the Pawnee, several groups of North America Indians lived in houses that were only partly below ground level. These are called pit houses.

Indians who lived in the northwest part of what is now California built square or rectangular pit houses. First they dug a hole that was three feet deep. Then they placed thick redwood or cedar planks upright around the walls of this pit. Next they built the upper wall of their homes from more upright planks that they notched and then tied together with vines. They set these walls back several feet from the edge of the pit. This formed a wide shelf where they could store their belongings. They used the lower level for cooking and eating. The final part of a pit home was the roof. Builders used planks for this, fitting them tightly together to keep out the rain. Some pit homes were as large as 30 feet long.

The Anasazi people of the Southwest, who were the ancestors of the Pueblo people, began building pit homes about 2,000 years ago. Other peoples of the Southwest, including the Hohokam, also lived in pit homes. They built these early homes over a square or circular hole that was three to four feet deep. Then they framed the upper part with large poles. Pit house builders finished by covering them with smaller poles and finally with earth. Later builders covered the outside of their homes with a thick layer of clay mud. This mixture of clay and mud is called adobe.

▲▼▲▼▲▼▲▼▲▼▲▼▲▼▲▼▲▼▲▼▲▼▲▼▲▼▲

EARTHEN ROOFS

Some Indian people of central California, including the Achomawi, Miwok, Maidu, and Pomo, heaped earth on their roofs. The Ntlakyapamuk (Thompson) and some other people of the Plateau region also built pit houses roofed with earth.

▼▲▼▲▼▲▼▲▼▲▼▲▼▲▼▲▼▲▼▲▼▲▼▲▼▲▼

HOGANS OF THE SOUTHWEST

The Dineh (Navajo) people of the Southwest lived in homes called hogans. They made their houses from wooden poles and earth. The earliest hogans were cone shaped. The Dineh made them by leaning together three forked poles and interlocking them at the top to form a tripod. Dineh builders sunk the bottoms of the posts into the ground. Then they leaned two more poles against this frame to mark the opening where the door would be.

Next, leaving a smoke hole, hogan builders set more poles on the frame

△▽△▽△▽△▽△▽△▽△▽△▽△▽△▽△▽△▽△▽△▽

HOME AT LAST
In the Dineh language the word *hogan* means "home place." The Dineh are Athapascan speakers. Their language has the same roots as that of the Indians who live in what is now the Yukon Territory of Canada. The Dineh people began moving southward in the 1200s. By the late 1400s they had settled in what came to be New Mexico and Arizona.

▽▲▽▲▽▲▽▲ ▽▲▽▲▽▲▽▲▽▲▽▲▽▲▽▲▽▲▽

to enclose the hogan. Then they filled the cracks with pieces of bark. Then the Dineh builders covered the entire hogan with about six inches of earth and packed it in place. Finally they covered their hogans with clay mud. They made a square entryway from wood and clay as well, and they covered the hogan door with a

Early hogans were covered with earth, which served as an insulator against heat and cold. Later the Navajo (Dineh) people began building the sides out of logs and covering only the roof with earth. The house in the background was considered a modern hogan when this picture was taken in 1938 at the Southern Navajo Agency. *(National Archives and Records Administration Pacific Alaska Region/Photograph No. NRIS-75-PAO50-NAVHOME4)*

hide. Like the dwellings of other Indian people, hogans had a central fire pit.

About 200 years later the Dineh began building larger six- and eight-sided hogans from cedar logs. The first builders of these hogans stacked the logs on top of one another horizontally. Later builders notched the logs on the ends and fitted them together in the style of log cabins. These hogans were about 20 feet across. They had domed roofs and were about 10 feet high. Indian builders made the roof from wooden logs, stacking shorter and shorter logs on top of one another to form a type of arch called a corbeled arch. As railroads were built nearby, the Dineh started building hogans from railroad ties.

Although many Dineh people on the Navajo Reservation today live in modern housing, families still use hogans for religious ceremonies. Sheepherders who must stay in remote areas also live in hogans while they watch their flocks.

ADOBE HOMES OF THE SOUTHWEST

In about A.D. 700, the Pueblo people began building aboveground rooms out of adobe in addition to the pit homes where they lived. These first adobe buildings were food storage warehouses. Later the Pueblo moved from their pit homes into small aboveground adobe homes. Then they began building clusters of them with shared walls. Next they began adding stories, or levels, to their dwellings.

Using adobe allowed them to eventually create large buildings with many rooms, referred to as *pueblos* by the Spaniards (*pueblo* is the Spanish word for village). Adobe was an excellent building material because it kept rooms cool during the daytime. At night the heat that the adobe walls had absorbed from the Sun radiated into the rooms. This was important in a climate where the daytime temperature tends to be hot and the nights are often chilly.

The most skillful Anasazi builders lived in the pueblos of Chaco Canyon in what is now New Mexico. The main village there is called Pueblo Bonito. It was

▲▽▲▽▲▽▲▽▲▽▲▽▲▽▲▽▲▽▲▽▲▽▲▽▲▽▲

KEEPING A TRADITION ALIVE

Even though they lived above ground, the Pueblo people remembered the houses of their ancestors. Adobe pueblos contained underground rooms called kivas where Pueblo people conducted religious ceremonies. These round rooms resembled the pit houses where they had lived years before.

▽▲▽▲▽▲▽▲▽▲▽▲▽▲▽▲▽▲▽▲▽▲▽▲▽▲▽

Adobe apartment complexes were common in the Southwest. Taos Pueblo, shown here, is occupied today. *(National Archives—College Park/Photograph No. NWDNS-79-AA-Q02)*

begun in about A.D. 850 as a complex of about 100 rooms. Pueblo Bonito was so well planned that modern archaeologists believe it was designed by ancient Anasazi architects, who were professional building planners.

To build Pueblo Bonito, the builders of Chaco Canyon first dug trenches and filled them with small rocks called rubble. Then they packed the trenches with adobe that hardened to form the foundation for the walls. Next the builders made walls from rough, flat stones. They used adobe for mortar to hold them together. Finally they covered this core with flat pieces of rock and plastered over them with more adobe. These walls tapered from three feet at the base to one foot at the top. An average room required about 50,000 tons of stone and 16,500 tons of clay. When the Anasazi wanted to add a new room, they attached new walls to old ones by interlocking the new stones with those in the walls they had already built.

Anasazi builders who lived in areas along the Rio Grande in what is now New Mexico often could not find enough suitable rock for their homes. They developed an alternative method of building. Rio Grande–area builders shaped adobe bricks by hand. When the bricks had dried, they set them atop each other to form walls. Then they smoothed over the surface with a finish coat of adobe. Anasazi builders in parts of what is now Arizona molded adobe bricks in wooden forms.

The Anasazi and later Pueblo builders supported the roofs of their pueblos with cedar beams. They covered the beams with branches and then grass. A final layer of adobe plaster on top of the roof sealed it against rain.

Today adobe architecture has come to be known as Santa Fe style and is popular throughout the Southwest. Modern builders, who must meet government building codes, find it more expensive to build with adobe than to construct frame houses. Often they plaster the exteriors of the standard homes they build with adobe because home buyers find the American Indian design pleasing.

WATTLE-AND-DAUB HOMES OF THE NORTH AMERICAN SOUTHEAST, MESOAMERICA, AND SOUTH AMERICA

Many groups of Indians throughout the Americas lived in wooden homes that they plastered with several layers of adobe. This method of building is called wattle and daub. *Wattle* and *daub* are terms for sticks and mud. These words come from England, where most people once built their houses in this way. The Spanish conquistadores called stick-and-mud construction *jacal*. In Peru it was called *quincha*.

Indians of the Southeast, including the Cherokee and Chickasaw, lived in wattle-and-daub houses during the winter. They built the frames for these homes by weaving tree branches and saplings together over a circular frame of upright poles. When they had finished, they plastered the frame with layers of clay mud, or adobe. They let each layer dry before applying the next. This made the house more waterproof. Southeastern builders wove the roofs of their houses with saplings and covered them with shingles made of bark.

Indian builders who lived in what is now Louisiana also built wattle-and-daub houses, mixing the mud with plant stalks and vines to make it stronger.

▽▲▽▲▽▲▽▲▽▲▽▲▽▲▽▲▽▲▽▲▽▲▽▲▽▲▽▲

SACBE
A Stronger Adobe

The Maya invented a very strong type of adobe plaster that they called *sacbe*. Builders burned pieces of limestone to obtain calcium oxide. They mixed this with sand, clay, and water. Sacbe was such a sturdy building material that in dry areas the Maya built houses with flat sacbe-covered roofs that were slightly tilted. When it rained, the water ran off the roofs and into a cistern, where they stored it for later use.

▽▲▽▲▽▲▽▲▽▲▽▲▽▲▽▲▽▲▽▲▽▲▽▲▽▲▽

Although the Maya and Aztec of Mesoamerica built large stone temples and public buildings, ordinary people lived in houses made from sticks and adobe. Ancient Maya people began building wattle-and-daub houses about 3,000 years ago. They made the stick and mud walls around an oval floor plan.

Maya builders topped the walls of their homes with thatched palmetto roofs. They built some houses with waist-high walls and very large roofs that slanted steeply. Both the overhang of the roof and its steep slope helped to keep the inside of Maya homes dry in a climate where it often rained.

Later the Maya began building wattle-and-daub homes that were rectangular. The Aztec also used this style for homes. Builders made a foundation platform by outlining the shape of the home with big stones. Then they filled this outline with dirt and next a layer of small stones. Finally they plastered the top of this foundation with adobe. This made a hard floor and kept homes high and dry in areas where it flooded.

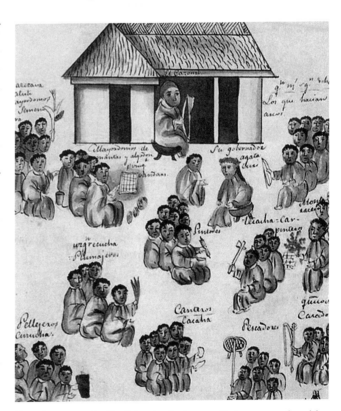

Most Aztec people lived in simple houses that were made with adobe and topped with thatched roofs. This copy of a 1540 drawing shows groups of people along with the tools of their trades. The original drawing was part of a book titled *Relación de las ceremonias y ritos y población y gobierno de los indios de la provincia de Mechoacán. (Library of Congress/Manuscript Division/Peter Force Collection)*

▲▽▲▽▲▽▲▽▲▽▲▽▲▽▲▽▲▽▲▽▲▽▲▽▲▽▲▽▲

RETURNING TO ANCIENT WAYS

In modern times, Native people of Peru were encouraged to build cheaper houses of rammed earth. Rammed earth is a mixture of sand, clay, and Portland cement that is formed into small blocks under pressure. The rammed-earth houses did not stand up to the severe earthquakes that are common in this part of South America. After an especially big earthquake in 1990, teams of architects worked to solve the problem of how to build quakeproof houses. They suggested that it would be safer for people to build quincha houses, a style invented by ancient Indian builders centuries before.

▽▲▽▲▽▲▽▲▽▲▽▲▽▲▽▲▽▲▽▲▽▲▽▲▽▲▽▲▽

The ancient people of what is now Peru built daub and wattle, or quincha, homes for centuries before the Spanish conquistadores arrived. Many of these had a circular floor plan. To build quincha homes, first they set large wooden poles in the ground. They spaced them at intervals around the circle. Then they wove saplings and thin branches between them. Finally they plastered the frame with adobe.

In addition to making quincha homes, Inca builders also used another method called *pirka*. Pirka is rough stone that has not been shaped. Using thick adobe and rough stone, they made walls. They plastered these walls with thinner adobe. In addition to making single-family homes with rough stones and adobe, builders often made one-story apartment buildings.

TIME LINE	
1000 B.C.	The Maya begin using wattle and daub, or jacal, for homes.
1 B.C.–A.D. 1	The Anasazi start living in pit homes in the desert Southwest.
A.D. 700	Mandan, Hidatsa, and Arikara Indians of the Great Plains begin building earth lodges along the Missouri River.
A.D. 700	The Anasazi move to aboveground homes that they make from adobe.
A.D. 1450–1680	Dineh people begin building hogans in the Southwest.

Public Buildings and Cities

4

Many of the 75 million to 100 million Indians living in the Americas before Europeans arrived on the continent lived in small villages. A number of them lived in larger towns and in enormous cities that were bigger than those of Europe at the time. For example, about 300,000 people lived in the Aztec capital of Tenochtitlán when the conquistadores under Hernán Cortés arrived in 1519. The combined population for the Tenochtitlán metropolitan area, which also included the cities of Tlatelolco and Texcoco, was about 1.2 million people. For comparison, modern cities of this size are San Diego, California, and Dallas, Texas.

Spanish conquistador Francisco Pizarro's secretary wrote in 1543 that the Inca capital city, Cuzco, had 100,000 houses when the first Spaniards arrived there 10 years earlier. Today historians estimate that about 250,000 people lived in the city and its suburbs. Modern cities that compare in population to Cuzco in 1533 are Trenton, New Jersey, and St. Petersburg, Florida.

▲▽▲▽▲▽▲▽▲▽▲▽▲▽▲▽▲▽▲▽▲▽▲▽▲▽▲▽

A CONTINENT OF CITY DWELLERS

More people lived in large pre-Columbian cities of America than lived in European cities at the time of conquest. By 1530, fewer than 30,000 people lived in Rome. In 1575 the population of Paris was 300,000. The population of London at that time was 180,000.

▼▲▼▲▼▲▼▲▼▲▼▲▼▲▼▲▼▲▼▲▼▲▼▲▼▲▼▲

The oldest major American city to be found so far is called Caral. It is located between the Pacific Ocean and the Andes in South America. Caral covered more than 200 acres and is believed to be at least 4,600 years old. The people who founded Caral were farmers. They built an irrigation system to water their pepper, bean, potato, and avocado plants. Archaeologists believe that the population of Caral numbered in the thousands.

American Indians began building Caral and other cities once farming became a dependable way of providing food. Planting and harvesting crops allowed people to live in one place instead of traveling in search of food in order to survive.

▲▽▲▽▲▽▲▽▲▽▲▽▲▽▲▽▲▽▲▽▲▽▲▽▲▽▲

LOOKING FOR CLUES

Today archaeologists continue to find pyramids, temples, and other evidence of abandoned South American and Mesoamerican cities. The blowing sands of Peru's dry coastal region have covered some of them. The jungles of the Mesoamerican lowlands have hidden others. Many more clues remain to be found.

▽▲▽▲▽▲▽▲▽▲▽▲▽▲▽▲▽▲▽▲▽▲▽▲▽▲▽

The materials that American Indians used to build their towns and cities varied depending on where they lived, but most American Indian cities were laid out around a civic plaza. This city center contained public buildings. Some of these were government buildings. Other buildings were used for religious ceremonies. In some places these included pyramids and temples. Cities in Mesoamerica had stone ball courts at their center. Some cities in the Southwest had ball courts as well. In the Southeast some groups of Indians also built their towns around flat playing fields. People traded goods on central plazas and often established formal marketplaces there.

ANCIENT CITIES OF SOUTH AMERICA

In addition to building the first cities in the Americas, the Indians who lived in what is now Peru were also the first American Indians to build pyramids. Caral, the oldest major city in the Americas, had six large stone pyramids at its center. Even though these are not the oldest pyramids of the Americas, one of them ranks among the largest in the world. It is nearly two football fields long and five stories tall. The outside of each pyramid was made from quarried stone (stone that was cut from the ground). The inside was filled with

▲▽▲▽▲▽▲▽▲▽▲▽▲▽▲▽▲▽▲▽▲▽▲▽▲▽▲▽▲

HOW DO ARCHAEOLOGISTS KNOW CARAL IS SO OLD?

To make huge platforms, the ancient builders of Caral carried cobblestones from the river in bags that were woven from reeds. They left the stones in these bags when they used them to fill the platform. Unlike rocks, the bags were organic material and contained carbon. Because of this they could be carbon dated. Carbon dating measures the amount of carbon-14 in organic materials to find out how old they are. Archaeologists believe the builders made the platforms in about 2627 B.C.

▽▲▽▲▽▲▽▲▽▲▽▲▽▲▽▲▽▲▽▲▽▲▽▲▽▲▽▲▽

smaller stones from a river near the town. In addition to the pyramids, Caral had three plazas at its center.

The ancient city of Caral had eight different neighborhoods. They were filled with stone palaces and adobe homes and apartment buildings. Archaeologists believe that Caral was constructed in two phases and that it required a great deal of planning. The neighborhoods appear to have been deliberately built instead of growing haphazardly.

Caral is only one of 18 known city sites in the region. El Aspero, a smaller town than Caral, was built in 3000 B.C. Located 14 miles away from the future site of Caral, it covered about 33 acres. Here ancient American Indian builders created the very first pyramids. They began by building small rooms of basalt blocks and used adobe mortar to hold the stones together. (Basalt is a volcanic rock.) Once the rooms were finished, they filled them with cobblestones from a river. Then they built more rooms and filled them, continuing the process until the pyramid was finished. The pyramids had rooms and courtyards at the

▲▽▲▽▲▽▲▽▲▽▲▽▲▽▲▽▲▽▲▽▲▽▲▽▲▽▲▽▲

THE OLDEST PYRAMIDS IN THE WORLD

South American builders began making pyramids years before the pyramids of Egypt were built. Archaeologists believe that the Egyptians built their first pyramid at Saqqara between 2886 and 2613 B.C. and constructed the famous Giza pyramids between 2589 and 2504 B.C.

▽▲▽▲▽▲▽▲▽▲▽▲▽▲▽▲▽▲▽▲▽▲▽▲▽▲▽▲▽

top. The builders plastered the sides of these pyramids with adobe and sculpted friezes (three-dimensional murals) on them. They painted them as well.

About 2,500 years after the first pyramids of South America were built, the Chavin people of the northern highlands of what is now Peru constructed more elaborate pyramids and ceremonial buildings at Chavin de Huantar. One of these buildings is called the Castillo today. Made from cut stone, it had three stories and contained stairs, rooms, and a unique ventilating system. Chavin builders made it with horizontal and vertical ventilation ducts instead of windows. This system still conveys fresh air throughout the Chavin temple today.

Inca stonemasons carved stones and set them carefully. They were such skilled builders that after hundreds of years it is still impossible to push a razor blade between the stones. *(Library of Congress, Prints and Photographs Division [LC-USZ62-97754])*

At about the same time, the Moche built Huaca del Sol (Pyramid of the Sun) near the northern coast of what is now Peru. Standing 98 feet tall and with a base that is 1,132 feet by 525 feet, it is the largest adobe building that pre-Columbian Indi-

▲▽▲▽▲▽▲▽▲▽▲▽▲▽▲▽▲▽▲▽▲▽▲▽▲▽▲

MAKING MODELS

Huge stone buildings took a great deal of planning. Before the ancient builders of the Andes set to work, architects made models of buildings called maquettes. A number of these models that are made of stone or pottery can be found in museums today.

▽▲▽▲▽▲▽▲▽▲▽▲▽▲▽▲▽▲▽▲▽▲▽▲▽▲▽

ans ever made. They built it from 140 million adobe bricks that they molded using forms. They inscribed each one of them with what archaeologists believe are the names of individual workers or teams of workers.

The Quechan-speaking people who lived in what is now Peru and the Inca, who followed them, were master stonemasons. The Inca used huge blocks that weighed as much as 20 tons each for some of their buildings. They obtained limestone, quartzite, granite, and basalt stone by quarrying, or mining it, from the ground.

First they chipped holes into the rock. Then they drove wooden wedges into the cracks and soaked them with water. When the water froze, the wedges expanded. This caused the rock to crack enough so that they could remove large pieces of it. The stonemasons used tools that were both rock and metal. Archaeologists have found bronze chisels that were used to quarry stone for the buildings at Machu Picchu, an Inca city high in the Andes mountains.

To shape the stone blocks, Inca stonemasons cut them with saws made from wires or fine copper or bronze blades. They used these with abrasives (gritty substances) and water. Some of the rocks in Inca buildings look as if they had been drilled with a bit. After they transported rocks to the construction site, Inca builders used rock hammers to further shape them. They used wires as tape measures to figure out exactly what size the stones needed to be. Then they polished the stones with sandstone or a sand-and-water mixture. Inca stonemasons also used a form of sliding ruler and a plumb line to set the stones so that no space remained between them. A plumb line is a string with a weight, or bob, on the end. It is used to find and mark a vertical line. They slid the stones into place using a thin layer of clay as a lubricant.

AMOJONADORESDESTEREINO.
VVACAVCHO.COMARAQVI
INGA   INGA

The public buildings and other works of the Inca were so large and complicated that many people were required to plan and complete them. Architects designed the projects and stonemasons built them.
(After Felipe Guamán Poma de Ayala, Nueva corónica y buen gobierno*)*

Builders laid out Cuzco, the Inca capital, on a grid pattern so that its streets were at right, or 90°, angles to each other. They paved these streets with basalt cobblestones. Stone-lined troughs that provided water for Cuzco's residents ran down the middle of the streets. The Inca also used copper pipes to transport hot and cold water to the sunken bathtubs in their bathhouses. One of the first Europeans to see Cuzco, Pedro Sancho de la Hoz, who was Pizarro's secretary, wrote in 1534: "Cuzco, because it is the capital city and the residence of the Inca nobles, is large enough and handsome enough to compare with any Spanish City."

ANCIENT CITIES OF MESOAMERICA

The Olmec, whose culture arose in about 1700 B.C., were the first big-city builders in Mesoamerica. Their largest urban centers, San Lorenzo, Tres Zapotecs, and La Venta, flourished between 1200 B.C. and 700 B.C. The Olmec had already developed a wide trading network by this time, and these cities served as trading centers.

Olmec builders worked with earth and basalt to construct elaborate temples and pyramids. At La Venta, which was once a ceremonial center and city of 18,000 people, the Olmec built a 112-foot-high pyramid. Olmec engineers used much the same method to construct pyramids as builders in pre-Columbian Peru did. They created rooms that they filled with rock, sand, and gravel. Then they repeated this process until the core of the pyramids was completed. Finally they finished the pyramids with an outer surface of basalt or granite, called a facing.

Long before the Romans built aqueducts to deliver water to the cities that they had established throughout Europe, the Olmec built stone water channels to provide water to buildings in their cities. They are the first American Indians known to have developed plumbing. Olmec engineers carved rectangular stone blocks that were three to five feet long into a U shape. These were used to transport water. They covered them with capstones to keep the water pure.

▲▽▲▽▲▽▲▽▲▽▲▽▲▽▲▽▲▽▲▽▲▽▲▽▲▽▲▽▲

THE MYSTERY OF THE CHIRPING PYRAMID

When people clap their hands or yell at the base of the Pyramid of Kukulán in the Maya city of Chichén Itzá, something strange happens. The echoes from the sounds they make are heard as chirping noises. Scientists believe that this is caused by the design of the stair steps leading to the top of the pyramid. Some researchers believe the chirps are accidental. Others think that the Maya deliberately designed the pyramid to make a sound similar to that made by the quetzal, a bird that they held sacred.

▽▲▽▲▽▲▽▲▽▲▽▲▽▲▽▲▽▲▽▲▽▲▽▲▽▲▽▲▽

The Maya, whose culture arose in Mesoamerica in about 1500 B.C., founded and constructed a number of cities on the Yucatán Peninsula of what is now Mexico. At their peak the Maya had more than 40 cities with from 5,000 to 50,000 residents in each one. These included Palenque, Tikal, Uxmal, and Chichén Itzá. All of the larger cities centered around pyramids.

Maya builders constructed square stone temples that sat atop pyramids made up of hundreds of steps. They also built large rectangular buildings near the temples. They made their public buildings from blocks of stone that they covered with a limestone plaster. This plaster set the stones in place and gave the buildings a whitewashed appearance. Maya builders applied limestone stucco, a thinned version of concrete, to wooden frames that they placed on temples and buildings in order to make them look taller without adding the weight of stone. The Maya finished the outer walls of these building with carved stone. They used stone roofs and invented the corbeled arch for the doorways of their stone buildings.

Mesoamerican architects designed buildings with corbeled arches such as this one at Uxmal. *(Latin American Library, Tulane University, Abby A. Gorin Collection)*

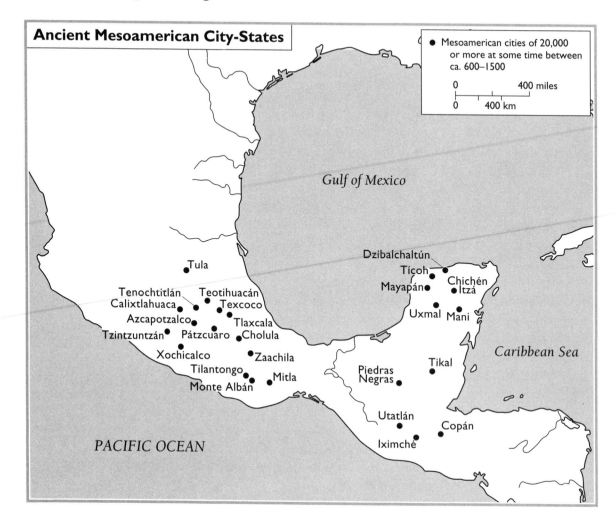

Ancient Mesoamerican City-States

● Mesoamerican cities of 20,000 or more at some time between ca. 600–1500

0   400 miles
0   400 km

Gulf of Mexico

Tula

Dzibalchaltún
Tícoh
Mayapán
Chichén Itzá
Uxmal   Mani

Tenochtitlán   Teotihuacán
Calixtlahuaca   Texcoco
Azcapotzalco
Tzintzuntzán   Pátzcuaro   Tlaxcala
Cholula
Xochicalco   Zaachila
Tilantongo
Monte Albán   Mitla

Piedras Negras
Tikal

Caribbean Sea

Utatlán
Iximché
Copán

PACIFIC OCEAN

Until the mid-20th century, archaeologists believed that ancient Mesoamericans were sloppy architects because many of the corners in their buildings do not form right angles. One example was a building called the Nunnery at Uxmal, a Maya city built between A.D. 800 and 1400. Then they discovered that builders had deliberately aligned the walls of this building with the rising and setting of stars and the planet Venus. Many other ancient Mesoamerican buildings were designed in a similar fashion.

The city of Teotihuacán, established near the northeast side of what is now called Lake Texcoco in central Mexico, is the oldest urban area in Mesoamerica. Founded in about A.D. 1, it spread to eventually cover eight square miles. By A.D. 500, between 100,000 and 200,000 people lived there. Teotihuacán contained three large pyramids and a plaza that was so large it could hold 100,000 people. Today scholars still know very little about the people who built this city. The word *Teotihuacán* in Nahuatl, the Aztec language, means "City of the Gods."

The people who built the city of Teotihuacán were expert pyramid builders. They made these monuments of adobe and then covered them with stone. One pyramid that they built in the highlands near the volcano Popocatépetl, stands 181 feet high and 1,300 feet

The Pyramid of the Magician was built by the Maya in Uxmal, in the Yucatán Peninsula. It is 100 feet tall and is really five pyramids with each one built over the others. The stairway of the pyramid faces the setting sun at the summer solstice. *(Latin American Library, Tulane University, Abby A. Gorin Collection)*

on a side—as long as three and a half football fields placed end to end. It contains nearly a million tons of adobe and is larger in volume than the Great Pyramid at Giza, the largest pyramid that the Egyptians built. It is so big that the Aztec later called it Tlachihualtépetl, which means "man-made mountain."

Centuries later, in A.D. 1325, the Aztec established the city of Tenochtitlán on the west side of Lake Texcoco. Today it is the site of Mexico City. Tenochtitlán, was the largest city in the Americas, with some 250,000 people living there. It was the capital of the Aztec Empire, which was established in about A.D. 1100 and ruled several million people. Tenochtitlán was filled with temples, palaces, schools, and a huge marketplace. Neighborhoods had their own smaller marketplaces that served the same purpose as strip malls today. This city also contained zoos and botanical gardens. Surrounded by lakes, it was the site of human-made islands, or chinampas, where farmers grew crops to feed the people who lived in Tenochtitlán.

Like other people of Mesoamerica, the Aztec built stone pyramids. They rebuilt them often. First they destroyed the existing temples atop pyramids. They then built a new pyramid and temple over

▲▼▲▼▲▼▲▼▲▼▲▼▲▼▲▼▲▼▲▼▲▼▲▼▲▼▲▼▲

THE SPANIARDS' REACTION TO TENOCHTITLÁN

When the conquistador Hernán Cortés and his men first saw Tenochtitlán and the roads leading from it, they could not believe their eyes. Bernal Díaz del Castillo, who wrote an account of Cortés's travels, noted: "Some of the soldiers among us who had been in many parts of the world, in Constantinople, and all over Italy and Rome, said that so large a marketplace and so full of people, and so well regulated and arranged, they had never seen before."

Cortés himself wrote: ". . . Amongst these temples there is one, the principal one, whose great size and magnificence no human tongue could describe, for it is so large that within the precincts, which are surrounded by a very high wall, a town of some five hundred inhabitants could easily be built."

▼▲▼▲▼▲▼▲▼▲▼▲▼▲▼▲▼▲▼▲▼▲▼▲▼▲▼▲▼

the rubble of the old one. Aztec stonemasons carved elaborate stone ornaments and coverings for their temples, which were more detailed than those of the Maya. As the Maya did, they carved wooden facades that rose above the roofs of the temples.

Like the Olmec and the Maya before them, the Aztec made cleanliness a priority. Many of their homes had personal restrooms. The Aztec built public restrooms as well. They constructed plaster-lined canals in their cities to carry human waste away and made other canals to bring fresh water to residents.

ANCIENT CITIES OF NORTH AMERICA

Indians of North America built a number of cities. These were generally smaller than those of the people of Mesoamerica and South America. They were also more varied in the way that they were laid out than those to the south.

Cities of the Southeast

Builders of the Mississippian Culture created a city called Cahokia eight miles east of the site of modern St. Louis, Missouri. During its peak, from A.D. 1050 to A.D. 1250, Cahokia had between 10,000 and 20,000 residents. The city center covered more than five square miles. Cahokia and its suburbs covered about 125 miles and contained more than 120 earthen mounds that supported civic buildings and the homes of the city's rulers. It was the center of a trade network that ranged from the Gulf Coast to the Great Lakes and from the Atlantic Coast to modern-day Oklahoma. Cahokia was the largest and most influential American Indian city in North America.

Most of the residents of Cahokia lived in single-family homes made of pole frameworks that they covered with thatched roofs and mat walls. They clustered these houses around small courtyards. These clusters were arranged around larger community plazas to form neighborhoods. These neighborhoods encircled the ceremonial buildings and earth works at Cahokia's center. Like modern cities, Cahokia had suburbs in addition to its thriving downtown. For reasons that are not known, the city began to decline in about A.D. 1200 and was virtually empty by A.D. 1400.

Mississippian people built earthworks throughout the Southeast, including locations in what are now Florida, Georgia, and Alabama. They also built smaller constructions as far north as what are now

▲▽▲▽▲▽▲▽▲▽▲▽▲▽▲▽▲▽▲▽▲▽▲▽▲▽▲▽▲

MOUND BUILDERS

Three groups of American Indians, the Adena, the Hopewell, and later the Mississippian Culture (actually a collection of distinct cultures), are called the Mound Builders. They created huge ceremonial earthworks along the Mississippi River in the central part of what is now the United States as well as in the Southeast. Early Mound Builders used the mounds as burial sites. In about 100 B.C. they began building very elaborate earthworks. Some were shaped like circles and others were squares or octagons. Mound Builders also made mounds shaped like huge snakes.

Later Mound Builders of the Mississippian Culture built mounds for their temples. The size of these earthworks was enormous. Monk's Mound, the largest pre-Columbian structure in North America, covered about 15 acres of land and was 100 feet tall. It took 22 million cubic feet of earth to build.

▽▲▽▲▽▲▽▲▽▲▽▲▽▲▽▲▽▲▽▲▽▲▽▲▽▲▽▲▽

Minnesota and Michigan. Some large Mississippian towns in North America besides Cahokia included:

- Moundville, which was built near what is now Tuscaloosa, Alabama, and had 10,000 residents
- Spiro, which was built in the eastern part of what is now Oklahoma on the Arkansas River, and covered almost 100 acres
- Etowah, which was built in northeast Georgia. (The people who lived there are considered the ancestors of the Creek people.)

Cities of the Southwest

The Anasazi, who are often considered the ancestors of the Pueblo people, built many settlements throughout the North American southwest desert. Pueblo Bonito, located in Chaco Canyon in what is now New Mexico, is one of the largest, most studied Anasazi cities. Chaco Canyon, which became a major trade center, was home to about 6,000 people.

The first permanent residents of Pueblo Bonito began living there about 900 B.C. By about A.D. 700, they began building adobe pueblos to make Pueblo Bonito. In the early 10th century Pueblo Bonito consisted of about 100 rooms. A century later it covered almost two acres and contained 800 rooms. At its highest point, the D-shaped pueblo was four stories high. The builders who made Pueblo Bonito and the smaller pueblos that surrounded it arranged the rooms around large courtyards that served as common areas. By about A.D. 1100 the Anasazi had built between 125 and 150 outlying pueblos. More than 400 miles of roads connected some of these smaller towns to Pueblo Bonito.

Casa Grande was built by the Hohokam people in about A.D. 1300. It is one of the largest prehistoric buildings made in North America. Today the ruins at Casa Grande Monument in Arizona are protected by a canopy to preserve them. *(Photographer: Grant/U.S. Department of the Interior National Park Service)*

The Hohokam people, whose culture arose in what is now Arizona in about 300 B.C., made huge adobe buildings that Spanish conquistadores compared to castles. Casa Grande (Spanish for "Big House"), built in about A.D. 1300 and located outside of what is now Phoenix, Arizona, is one of these. Casa Grande is four stories tall and took 1,500 cubic yards of soil to build.

Hohokam builders mixed mud to the proper consistency in large holes they dug in the ground. They then piled it up, or "puddled" it, by hand in 26-inch layers. They allowed each layer to dry before making the next one. The walls that they made are four feet thick at the base.

After nearly 700 years, the walls of Casa Grande are weathered but still stand. This is because the original architects used caliche for the adobe. Caliche is a soil layer in which earth particles have been bonded by carbonates of calcium or magnesium. This causes the adobe to harden, almost like cement, as it dries.

Archaeologists do not know the exact purpose of Casa Grande and other huge Hohokam buildings but believe that they were designed to protect cities against attack. Window openings in upper levels of Casa Grande are aligned to the position of the Sun at the time of equinox and at solstices, so it could have also served as an observatory.

Cities of the Northeast

Many Indians of the Northeast lived in large villages and small cities. One Huron village that was located near modern Toronto had 45 to 50 longhouses and covered 15 acres in 1500. At least 2,000 people lived there. In 1535 French explorer Jacques Cartier reported that 3,600 people lived in 50 bark longhouses in Hochelaga, an Iroquois town near what is now Montreal.

During the early part of European colonization, the villages of the Northeast continued to grow. By the late 1600s the Iroquois settlement of Gannagaro in modern-day Ontario County, New York, consisted of 150 longhouses with thousands of residents. By this time the Iroquois had built at least 25 major towns. One of the largest was a two-village settlement called Cahiague between Lake Simcoe and the Georgian Bay in Ontario. It was made up of 200 longhouses and had about 4,000 people living there. As European colonists claimed more land, most large Indian towns of the Northeast were either destroyed or abandoned.

TIME LINE

3000 B.C.	Early people of what is now Peru build El Aspero, the oldest city found in the Americas.
2600 B.C.	Early people of what is now Peru build Caral, the oldest major city in the Americas.
1200 B.C.	The Olmec build their cities on the Yucatán Peninsula of what is now Mexico.
900 B.C.	Chavin builders begin work on Chavin de Huantar just north of what is now Lima, Peru.
100 B.C	Mound Builders of North America begin building earthworks.
A.D. 1	Ancient people of what is now central Mexico establish Teotihuacán.
A.D. 700	The Anasazi start building Pueblo Bonito in what is now New Mexico.
A.D. 1000	Inca stonemasons begin building large cities of stone in what is now Peru.
A.D. 1050–A.D. 1250	Cahokia, the largest city of the Mound Builders, is at its peak.
A.D. 1300	The Hohokam build Casa Grande near what is now Phoenix, Arizona.
A.D. 1325	The Aztec establish Tenochtitlán on Lake Texcoco.

5

Clothing from Hides

The clothing that American Indians made depended on the materials that were available to them where they lived. Because clothing needed to protect them from the elements, they invented styles of clothing that were practical for the weather where they lived. Indians who lived in cold climates needed to keep warm, so they tended to wear many layers of clothing and designed clothing styles that trapped body heat. Those who lived in tropical or semitropical parts of the Americas tended to wear very little clothing. The garments that they did wear were light in weight.

Throughout the Americas Indian people used animal skins to make both clothing and footwear. The earliest American Indians made their clothing from leather. Most of what is known today about the hide clothing that Indians wore centers on North American Indians. Because leather disintegrates over long periods of time, for the most part historians can only know what Indian people wore at the time of European contact. Native people of Mesoamerica and South America knew how to tan leather, but by the time of European contact they made most of their clothing from cloth.

TANNING LEATHER

Before animal skins have been processed into leather, they are not very useful for making clothing. Rawhide, the untreated skin of animals with the fur removed, is stiff and has sharp edges. Untreated animal skins also have a tendency to rot quickly. Indians of the Americas invented a process to make animal skins soft and pliable. They used the hides they had tanned to create clothing that was practical and comfortable.

Some of the animal skins that North American Indians used for clothing were those of elk, deer, caribou, seal, buffalo, and beaver. These were the same animals that they hunted for food. The men were in charge of hunting the animals. The women were usually responsible for tanning hides and making clothing from the leather.

Indian hide tanners used the natural oils present in the brains of the animals that they hunted in order to soften hides. This method, called brain tanning, also produces leather that is both soft and water resistant. Invented by the Paleo-Indians thousands of years ago, brain tanning is still practiced by American Indians today. Brain-tanned leather is of such high quality that it is considered a luxury leather in modern times.

To brain-tan a hide, Indians first skinned an animal they had hunted and killed. Removing the animal's skin required both care and skill. Once they had removed an animal's skin, Indians washed it first to clean away the blood. Next they soaked the animal skin in water to loosen the fur. Sometimes they added wood ashes to speed the process. Indians of many tribes would bury an animal skin for a few days after it had soaked to make the fur easier to remove. Then Indian tanners laced the animal skin to a frame made of wood in order to stretch it. Some tribes staked the hide on the ground, rather than on a frame, in order to make it taut.

Once they had stretched the hide, Indian tanners used tools called scrapers to carefully

This Anishinabe woman from the Red Lake Agency in Minnesota is giving a last scraping to deer hides before she tans them. Every bit of hair and muscle tissue had to be removed. This photo was taken in 1939. *(National Archives and Records Administration Central Plains Region/Photograph No. NRE-75-RL[PHO]-1077)*

remove the fur and the top layer of skin. They made scrapers from bone, antler, or stone. After they had finished, they turned the skin over and fleshed the underside by scraping away the pieces of muscle and tissue that remained there. Fleshing a hide required a great deal of skill. It was important for tanners to use just the right pressure so that they did not cut the skin. Once they had scraped and fleshed the hide, they soaked it overnight in water.

The next day Indian tanners coated the skin with a mixture of mashed animal brains and water. Sometimes tanners added other things to this mixture such as yucca, soaproot, or cornmeal. When the skin they were working on had softened enough so that it could be folded, they dipped it in a container of brain solution and kneaded it so that the brains and water would soak deeply into the hide.

▲▼▲▼▲▼▲▼▲▼▲▼▲▼▲▼▲▼▲▼▲▼▲▼▲▼▲▼▲▼

WHY BRAINS?

Both animals and people have oil glands in their skin that keep it flexible. Sometimes, if their skin is dry, it chaps and becomes cracked. When this happens to people, they use moisturizer that contains fats or oil in order to soften their skin. Brain tanning works the same way.

Skins of animals that are no longer living dry out quickly. Brains contain a great deal of fatty tissue. (The myelin sheath, which serves as an electrical insulator on certain types of nerve cells in the brain, is mostly made from a type of fat.) When the fat is worked into an animal skin, it makes the skin flexible and water resistant.

▼▲▼▲▼▲▼▲▼▲▼▲▼▲▼▲▼▲▼▲▼▲▼▲▼▲▼▲▼▲▼

Not all Indians used animal brains when they made leather. Some of them used the bone marrow or livers of the animals that they hunted instead. Indians of the Southwest used mashed jojoba berries or saguaro cactus seeds. American Indians who lived in the woodlands of northeastern North America sometimes soaked hides in a mixture of hemlock and oak bark. These two barks are high in a substance called tannin. They soaked and worked the skin over a period of three months before it was finally finished. The

▲▼▲▼▲▼▲▼▲▼▲▼▲▼▲▼▲▼▲▼▲▼▲▼▲▼▲▼▲

FUR ROBES

Tanned hides with the fur left on them are called robes. When Indians wanted to make a robe, they did not soak or bury the animal skin before they fleshed the underside, the side without the fur. After they finished scraping the hide, they covered the underside with a paste made of brains and worked the solution into the skin in order to keep it soft.

▼▲▼▲▼▲▼▲▼▲▼▲▼▲▼▲▼▲▼▲▼▲▼▲▼▲▼▲▼

Inuit used fish oils when they made leather. Oil-tanned leather has the look and feel of chamois.

After Indian tanners had wrung the tanning solution out of the skin, the real work began. They worked the hide until it dried by pulling and stretching it in order to make the fibers expand and become more flexible. Sometimes Indian women chewed on hides as they dried in order to break down the fibers and make them softer.

A finished buckskin was white and had the feel of flannel, a soft cloth. At this point, if it got wet and then dried, the animal skin would get hard again. American Indians discovered that when smoke penetrated the fibers of leather, a tanned hide would remain soft and pliable even in rainy weather. They smoked hides by throwing punky, or rotten, wood onto a fire and placing the hides over the smoke for several hours until they turned a golden brown color.

American Indian women began sewing leather to make clothing by first punching holes in it with bone awls. Then they sewed pieces together with sinew, the tough tissue that connects animals' muscles to their bones. The longest pieces of sinew, those that run along an animal's backbone, were the most useful for this.

After American Indians tanned hides, they smoked the leather so that it would remain soft and flexible. This photo of an Iroquois man smoking a hide was taken in Grand River, Quebec, in 1914. (*National Archives of Canada/National Museums of Canada Collection/Photograph No. PA-175362/*)

▲▼▲▼▲▼▲▼▲▼▲▼▲▼▲▼▲▼▲▼▲▼▲▼▲▼▲

NEEDLES

The oldest bone needle found in the United States was invented by Paleo-Indians living in what is now Washington State. It has been dated to 8000 B.C. South American metalworkers who lived near the Andes Mountains invented a copper sewing needle between A.D. 800 and A.D. 1100.

▼▲▼▲▼▲▼▲▼▲▼▲▼▲▼▲▼▲▼▲▼▲▼▲▼▲▼

▲▽▲▽▲▽▲▽▲▽▲▽▲▽▲▽▲▽▲▽▲▽▲▽▲▽▲

WHY A DOLLAR IS CALLED A BUCK

New England colonists often used buckskins instead of money to trade for other items they needed. They shortened the word *buckskins* to *bucks*. Many people still use *buck* as slang for a one-dollar bill.

▽▲▽▲▽▲▽▲▽▲▽▲▽▲▽▲▽▲▽▲▽▲▽▲▽▲▽

Indian women guided the sinew through the holes with very thin bone needles. Women of some tribes used fish bones for needles.

When the European colonists arrived in North America, many American Indians wore brain-tanned garments sewn with sinew. The colonists recognized that these garments were both practical and comfortable, so they, too, began wearing brain-tanned clothing. During the Revolutionary War George Washington ordered buckskins for his troops.

Not only did the colonists often adopt this style of clothing, but brokers began shipping buckskin that Indians had made to Europe. At first American buckskin was used to make work clothes for tradespeople. By the mid-1700s it became popular among wealthy people, who wore buckskin breeches, as well as for hunting and riding gear. Between 1755 and 1773, more than 2.5 million pounds of buckskin made by the Creek and Cherokee were shipped to England from Savannah, Georgia.

LEATHER CLOTHING OF THE ARCTIC AND SUBARCTIC

The Inuit of the Arctic used the hides of seals, polar bears, foxes, squirrels, caribou, and even birds to make parkas. Some people who lived in the subarctic also made parkas. This loose-fitting, hooded style of jacket was made and worn by Native people from Greenland to Alaska, long before contact with Europeans. It fit loosely so that the wearer could pull his or her arms into the body of the jacket to warm them. Some parkas reached to mid-thigh and some hung as low as ankle length.

In winter the Inuit and the people of the subarctic wore two parkas. They put the first parka on with the fur facing in. The fur on the outer parka faced out. This layering allowed for air circulation and also provided better insulation. Caribou fur, one of the most popular parka liners, has hollow hairs that trap body heat next to the wearer's skin even in the coldest of temperatures. Parka makers also lined the garments with bird skins with the feathers left in place. This produced

Although the parka's design is an American Indian invention, the word *parka* is an English version of a Russian word, given to this unique style of jacket.

the same effect as modern down jackets. When parka makers constructed the entire garment from bird skins, which are very thin, they insulated the seams with ermine, caribou, or mountain goat fur. The fur served as a barrier against the wind.

Often hunters dressed in caribou fur parkas, not only to keep warm, but also to pursue caribou. Seal hunters often wore sealskin parkas while hunting. George Best, who served as an officer on Englishman Martin Frobisher's expeditions to locate the Northwest Passage in the late 16th century, wrote of the Inuit, "They are good fishermen, and in their small boats, and disguised with their sealskin coats, they deceive the fish, who take them for fellow seals rather than deceiving men."

When clothing becomes wet and the water evaporates, this rapidly lowers the wearer's body temperature. To keep their jackets dry, some Inuit made parka covers from chinook salmon (king salmon) skins. Others sewed parka covers from whale bladders, intestines, or the skin of a whale's tongue.

The Inuit often lined parkas and their hoods with fur. Because the fur trapped warm air next to the body, these garments kept people warm even in the coldest temperatures. (Lomen Bros., Photographer/Library of Congress, Prints and Photographs Division [LC-USZ62-330797])

The Inuit of the Arctic invented the parka, a style of jacket worn today. They often made these jackets from caribou or seal skin but used other materials as well, including bird skins. (U.S. Bureau of Ethnography)

The Inuit designed women's parkas slightly differently than those made for men. They made women's parkas with a large inside pouch on the back for carrying an infant. The baby was held in place by a strap around the mother's chest. Mothers carried their children in this baby carrier for the first two to three years of their lives. Large hoods on women's parkas allowed air to circulate and wide shoulders allowed a mother to move the child to breast-feed it without exposing it to the cold.

Waterproof parkas that the Inuit made from the bladders or intestines of sea mammals kept fishermen dry and warm. In this picture the fisherman is holding a toy boat he has made for his son. *(Lomen Bros., Photographer/Library of Congress, Prints and Photographs Division [LC-USA62-130984])*

Although European contact brought many changes to Inuit life, hunters kept their parkas and parka covers, long after the introduction of trade cloth to the north. Parkas worked better at keeping out cold and dampness than factory-made clothing. Today non-Indian people have adopted this style of jacket. It is a popular and fashionable winter-wear design throughout the world.

The Inuit people also invented many other types of clothing that are common throughout the world today. Paleo-Indians of the Arctic were making tailored trousers as early as 15,000 B.C. Both Inuit men and women of the Arctic and subarctic wore fur trousers. They made them by sewing two leggings together by running a seam up the front and the rear. Beneath their trousers, Inuit people wore briefs made from skins. In winter they wore long underwear made from hides.

On their feet the Inuit and people of the Subarctic wore mukluks, soft boots made from reindeer skin or sealskin. They made waterproof mukluks from chinook salmon skins. Inside the mukluks they wore socks made of thin leather. They covered these with woven

▲▽▲▽▲▽▲▽▲▽▲▽▲▽▲▽▲▽▲▽▲▽▲▽▲▽▲

AN INFLATABLE WET SUIT

When the Inuit hunted whales or seals from their hide boats, they wore a special garment that was made of sealskins with the hair removed. This one-piece suit covered the wearer from head to toe. It had a hood that could be tightened around the face with a drawstring so that it was watertight and airtight. When it was filled with air and the openings were securely closed, it could keep hunters afloat in the water for several hours.

▼▲▽▲▽▲▽▲▽▲▽▲▽▲▽▲▽▲▽▲▽▲▽▲▽▲▽

grass socks or wadded grass liners that kept their feet warm in sub-zero temperatures.

To keep from slipping on the snow, Inuit people attached pieces of hide, bone, or ivory to the bottom of their mukluks to provide traction. To travel across snow, the Inuit and other tribes who lived in the north also used snowshoes made from strips of hide stretched over a wooden frame. Snowshoes helped them walk on the surface of the snow without sinking.

LEATHER CLOTHING OF THE NORTHEAST, SOUTHEAST, PLAINS, AND PLATEAU

Many North American Indians who lived south of the Arctic and Subarctic also wore leather clothing. Although different tribes developed unique styles, the basic design of their clothing was often quite similar from tribe to tribe.

In general men and boys wore breechclouts. These were rectangular pieces of tanned hide that they draped between their legs. The hide they used most often for this purpose was deerskin because it was soft yet strong. Men of some tribes tied the sides of their breechclouts together at their waists with strips of leather. Men of other tribes looped the ends of the breechclouts over a larger strip of leather that served as a belt to keep them in place. When the front and back flaps of their breechclouts were long, they often fringed and decorated them. Men of some tribes wrapped a hide around their waists so that it resembled a kilt.

American Indian men and boys sometimes wore leggings as well. These coverings protected their legs from the cold and from sharp branches and thorns. In the Northeast, Indians made men's leggings from long, rectangular pieces of leather that were tied down the back. Worn with a breechclout, they resembled trousers. Indian men of the Great Plains wore similar leggings, but they were often tied at the sides. In the winter, men of the Great Basin and Plateau wore leggings as well.

In cool weather Indian men also wore simple hide shirts that resembled ponchos. When the weather turned cold, they wore robes that were made from hides with the fur left on them. These large capes had leather strips, or thongs, attached to them that tied at the neck. Indians of the Northeast and Southeast used bear, raccoon, wildcat, elk, and deer skins for robes. Because buffalo were

American Indians of the Great Basin, Plateau region, and Southwest all wore socks to keep their feet warm or to protect their feet from blisters caused by their footwear. They made socks from soft, thin hides or from woven grass.

The beaded dance outfit that this Plains Indian girl named Annie wore for this 1937 picture was based on a traditional two-hide dress. (Indians did not use glass beads until after contact with Europeans.) Rather than trimming the extra hide from a garment, American Indians cut it into fringe. *(National Archives and Records Administration Central Plains Region/Photograph No. NRE-75-PRSERIES208-621)*

so plentiful and winters were so fierce on the Great Plains, Indians who lived there wore thick, furry buffalo robes in the winter. Indian men of California tribes sometimes wore thinner robes that were made from many rabbit skins sewn together.

Indian women and girls who lived where the weather was warm wore wraparound skirts and capes or ponchos made from deerskin. In areas where the weather was cooler they wore leather dresses. Women of the Northeast wore knee-length dresses made of two hides that they had sewed down the sides. They sewed leather shoulder straps at the top. Their dresses had sleeves that were tied to these straps and could be removed.

Women of the Plains wore similar dresses made of two skins. These dresses were made by sewing one hide up the side to form the skirt. Indian women made the tops and sleeves of their dresses by folding another hide lengthwise and cutting an opening at the center of the fold for the neck. The ends of this hide formed the dress sleeves. They finished the dress by sewing the skirt to the top.

Most of the time, Indian clothing makers did not trim the hides when they sewed seams. Instead they cut the excess leather into

ROBES FOR WOMEN AND CHILDREN

Like Indian men did, women and children wrapped themselves in robes in the wintertime. In some tribes women and children wore robes made from pieces of rabbit skin sewn together because rabbit fur was the softest available to them.

▲▽▲▽▲▽▲▽▲▽▲▽▲▽▲▽▲▽▲▽▲▽▲▽▲▽▲

A PRACTICAL STYLE

Fur trappers and traders and colonists on the American frontier began wearing buckskin trousers shortly after contact with Indians. Hide trousers were more practical than hose and short pantaloons or knickers made from cloth, which were the standard dress of Europeans at that time.

▽▲▽▲▽▲▽▲▽▲▽▲▽▲▽▲▽▲▽▲▽▲▽▲▽▲▽

fringe. Sometimes if the hide they were using was not large enough to allow for fringing, they sewed a band of fringe onto the garment when they had finished it. Another way they made long fringe on their clothing was to tie thongs onto shirts, dresses, and along the side seam of leggings.

The style of fringe that Indian people wore depended on the tribe. The Kiowa and Comanche who lived on the southern plains wore long, twisted fringe that they gathered into bunches. Their long heel fringes erased their tracks when they walked. The Blackfeet, Cheyenne, and Crow of the northern plains also tended to wear long, twisted fringe on their garments. Other northern plains people wore long, straight fringe. American Indians of the eastern woodlands generally wore garments with shorter fringes that would not become tangled in underbrush that grew in the forests where they hunted.

European fur trappers, traders, and frontiersmen copied the way North American Indian men dressed. In the early 1800s they wore shirts and leggings that had so much fringe that some Indians called them the "fringe people." Today modern fashion designers often decorate leather garments, such as jackets, with fringe.

Mountain men adopted the clothing styles of American Indians, including leather garments and fringe. This photo of California trapper Seth Kinman was taken in the mid-1800s. *(Library of Congress, Prints and Photographs Division [LC-USZ62-116289])*

Indians of the Northeast wore cuffed moccasins. The Huron moccasin shown in the photograph detail above is decorated with beads and ribbons. Before contact with Europeans, American Indians decorated their moccasins with porcupine quills, rather than beads or ribbon. (*Marius Barbeau, Photographer/National Museum of Canada Collection/National Archives of Canada/Photograph No. PA-175385*)

Like other people of the world, American Indians invented shoes to protect their feet from cold temperatures and sharp objects. A number of Indian people in North America wore moccasins. They sewed moccasins from bison, moose, elk, or deer hides. Although most moccasins were low topped, Indian people could quickly make them into high tops by attaching leggings to them. In winter Indians lined moccasins with fur or grass to provide insulation. People of the Southwest and the Great Plains wore moccasins with hard soles made from rawhide they shaped to fit the bottoms of their feet. This protected their feet from the thorny plants that grew where they lived. Tribes that lived in the Northeast of North America occasionally tied fur strips to the bottom of their moccasins in order to help them walk on ice.

Moccasin styles worn by different groups of Indians were so unique that trackers could tell what tribe another Indian belonged to by studying his or her footprints. For this reason, sometimes American Indians tied animal tails or fringe to the heels of their moccasins to brush away their tracks as they walked.

6

Clothing from Fiber

Indians of the Americas used both plant and animal fibers to make their clothing. Those who lived in some areas gathered or hunted most of the fibers that they needed, such as cedar bark, cattail leaves, and buffalo wool. Other Indians raised both plants and animals for fiber, including agave, cotton, alpacas, and llamas.

PLANT FIBERS THAT AMERICAN INDIANS USED FOR CLOTHING

American Indians who lived in the Northwest made some of the clothing they wore from bark that they gathered from cedar trees. Indians of the Northeast and Southeast gathered cattail leaves, milkweed, nettles, and other fibers. Even though they made most of their clothing from hides, they used these fibers to make bags and belts. They also wove tumplines, straps that they used for carrying loads and bulky items.

Indians of the desert Southwest and Mesoamerica planted and harvested agave for fiber. (This plant is called *maguey* in Spanish.) They used the agave that they grew for food and medicine as well as for clothing. Processing fiber from these plants so that it could be spun into thread for weaving was a difficult job. First the harvesters, who were usually men, cut the long, sword-shaped leaves from the plants. Next they heated them over a fire in order to soften their tough outer covering. After they soaked the leaves until they had begun to decay, they dried them. Finally they scraped the pulp from the leaves and beat the fibers with paddles in order to soften them more.

▲▽▲▽▲▽▲▽▲▽▲▽▲▽▲▽▲▽▲▽▲▽▲▽▲▽▲▽▲▽▲

SANDALS

Indians of the Southwest and Mesoamerica used agave and yucca fibers to make braided ropes that they used to create sandals. Paleo-Indians of Southwest made the oldest sandals that have been found in North America. They made them in about 7000 B.C.

American Indians used the fiber ropes that they made to form soles and straps. Aztec sandal makers designed sandals that were held in place with straps similar to those of modern flip-flops. They also made sandals with long straps that criss-crossed the wearer's calves. The Olmec, whose culture arose in the Yucatán Peninsula in about 1700 B.C., coated the soles of the fiber sandals that they made with rubber.

▼▲▽▲▽▲▽▲▽▲▽▲▽▲▽▲▽▲▽▲▽▲▽▲▽▲▽▲▽▲▽

American Indians who lived in what are now Peru and Mexico used cotton for their clothing. Cotton is a plant that produces a clump of fiber around its seeds. At first they gathered fiber from wild cotton plants. Archaeologists, scientists who study the past, have found mummies in Peru that were wrapped in cotton cloth. These mummies are between 7,000 and 8,000 years old.

Between 3500 and 2300 B.C. Indian people of the Andes and Mesoamerica began planting and harvesting cotton. As much as 10 percent of the fields that ancient farmers of Peru planted were filled with cotton. The Maya, whose culture arose in about 1500 B.C. in Mesoamerica, grew cotton in household garden plots, as well as in village fields.

The Hohokam people in the Southwest began growing cotton in irrigated fields about 1,500 years ago. Their culture flourished in the desert of what is now Arizona starting in about 300 B.C. Later the Anasazi people began to cultivate cotton as well. The Zuni also grew cotton. Ancient farmers of the Southwest developed a

Aztec men who were not part of the ruling class wore simple tunics that were made from agave or cotton. They also wore sandals that were made from agave fibers that had been braided and sewn together. This detail is from a picture that was drawn in 1525. *(Library of Congress, Prints and Photographs Division [LC-USZ62-124461])*

▲▼▲▼▲▼▲▼▲▼▲▼▲▼▲▼▲▼▲▼▲▼▲▼▲▼▲

COLORFUL COTTON

American Indians raised cotton in many colors, including beige, brown, mauve, and rust. This amazed one Spanish author, Bernabe Cobo, who wrote a book called *History of the New World* in 1653. He had never seen colored cotton plants and thought that American Indians dyed the cotton plants while they were still growing in their fields. Other European writers copied his mistake.

▼▲▼▲▼▲▼▲▼▲▼▲▼▲▼▲▼▲▼▲▼▲▼▲▼▲▼

variety called *Gossypium hopi,* or Hopi cotton, that was adapted to their climate. It has the shortest growing season of any variety in the world.

ANIMAL FIBERS THAT AMERICAN INDIANS USED FOR CLOTHING

Thousands of years ago people who lived in the Andes of South America began making garments from the silky wool that they obtained from vicuñas. These animals are the smallest members of the camel family and are related to llamas and alpacas. Their wool is long, soft, and shiny. Because vicuñas can run fast, Indian people worked together to frighten vicuña herds so that they would run into rope traps. When they had trapped the animals, they sheared, or cut, the wool from the animals, with sharp stone knives.

The Indian people of the Andes domesticated, or tamed, llamas and alpacas about 4,000 years ago. Alpacas weigh about twice as much as vicuñas and stand about three feet tall. Llamas are larger. The wool these animals produce has strong fibers. Because alpaca fibers are hollow, they provide good protection against the cold. Clothing that the Indians wove from alpaca wool was soft and light. Llama fibers produced coarser garments.

North American Indians also used a variety of

▲▼▲▼▲▼▲▼▲▼▲▼▲▼▲▼▲▼▲▼▲▼▲▼▲▼▲

LUXURY WOOL

After the Inca created their empire in about A.D. 1000, only the nobility were allowed to wear cloth made from vicuña fleece. Common people caught wearing such garments were executed. Today vicuña wool brings about $225 a pound in the world market.

▼▲▼▲▼▲▼▲▼▲▼▲▼▲▼▲▼▲▼▲▼▲▼▲▼▲▼

▲▼▲▼▲▼▲▼▲▼▲▼▲▼▲▼▲▼▲▼▲▼▲▼▲▼▲▼

WOOL IN MANY SHADES

The people of the Andes bred alpacas to produce a variety of colors of wool. Alpaca wool comes in more than 20 natural shades, from white to silver, rose gray, brown, burgundy, and black. They used these different colors of wool to make designs in the cloth they wove.

▼▲▼▲▼▲▼▲▼▲▼▲▼▲▼▲▼▲▼▲▼▲▼▲▼▲▼

animal fibers, including buffalo wool, to weave into belts. Indians of the Great Basin and the Southwest cut rabbit skins into strips and wove them into blankets to use as robes in cold weather. Some tribes of the Southwest wove feathers into their blankets to provide beauty and insulation against cold nights. In both the Southwest and the Northeast, Indians collected the wool from wild mountain sheep for making blankets.

The Salish people of the Northwest bred dogs for the fiber they produced. These dogs had thick white fur. The women who bred them kept their dogs on islands off the coast so that they would not mate with hunting dogs and produce offspring with fur that was not white. Salish women sheared the dogs' fur with sharp knives that they made from mussel shells. They wove this fur into belts and blankets. When they wanted patterns in their weaving, they added bear fur or the fur from dark-colored dogs into the design.

WEAVING AND WOVEN CLOTHING

Many Indians made cloth without looms. This method is called finger weaving. Braiding, knotting, knitting, looping, and netting are all types of finger weaving. Indians usually used finger weaving to make small items like belts and bags.

Before American Indians could make sewn clothing from fiber, they needed to turn that fiber into large pieces of fabric, or cloth. American Indians invented looms in order to weave these pieces of cloth. Looms are made up of crossbars over which weavers string warp threads, the lengthwise threads in cloth. These bars keep the threads tight so that they will not tangle and the cloth will turn out flat and even.

Weavers then use tools called heddles to raise the warp threads so that cross threads can be easily passed between them. These cross threads are called woof, or weft, threads. Once they pass a woof thread between the warp threads, weavers push it firmly in place with a tool that is called a batten, or beater.

American Indians created beautiful and useful material on their looms. The fabrics that they made ranged from thin gauzes to sturdy double cloth. They wove designs, such as stripes and checks, into the cloth that they made.

The most popular loom in the Americas was the backstrap loom. It was used by weavers of the South American Andes as well as by weavers in Mesoamerica and the North American Southwest. After a weaver had strung warp threads between large horizontal sticks, he or she tied one end of the loom to a tree or post to anchor it. The weaver then tied the other end of the loom to his or her waist or hips with a leather strap—the backstrap. By leaning forward or backward, the weaver, usually a woman, controlled the tightness of the warp threads. Backstrap looms, which were about 20 inches wide, worked well for making fairly wide strips of cloth that could be sewn together.

Some American Indian weavers invented another type of loom for making even larger pieces of cloth. Weavers in the South American Andes, Mesoamerica, and the North American Southwest and Northwest made blankets on large looms with wooden frames. They wore these blankets as robes.

Backstrap looms like this one, originally drawn by Indian artist and historian Felipe Guamán Pomo de Ayala in the early 1600s, were used by weavers in South America to make cloth. (Nueva corónica y buen gobierno)

Weaving and Woven Clothing of South America

Weavers who lived in a dry part of what is now Peru made the oldest woven cloth that has been found in the Americas. These weavers used backstrap looms to make strips of cloth. They used this cloth to wrap mummies about 8,000 to 5,000 years ago.

By about 2,000 years ago the Chavin people, who lived in what is now Peru, had become expert weavers. To turn cotton into cloth, first they twisted it into yarn using a drop spindle. A weaver made a drop spindle by putting a weight onto a short, smooth stick. To start spinning yarn, the weaver twisted a length of cotton with his or her fingers and tied it to the stick. Then holding the yarn that he or she had twisted, the weaver let the spindle drop so that it hung suspended. Next while the weaver held the cotton fiber in one hand, the weaver began rolling the stick part of the spindle on the top of his or

△▽△▽△▽△▽△▽△▽△▽△▽△▽△▽△▽△▽△▽△▽△▽△▽△

WEAVING
A 10,000-Year Tradition
Some scientists who study the past believe that weaving might have begun in what is now Ecuador as early as 10,000 years ago. Because cloth decays in damp climates, researchers must rely on murals or statues that show people wearing cloth clothing to learn the history of weaving. They also use ancient pottery fragments that Indians decorated by pressing cloth into the clay to make a pattern.

▽△▽△▽△▽△▽△▽△▽△▽△▽△▽△▽△▽△▽△▽△▽△▽△▽

her thigh with the other hand. The rolling motion twisted the fiber into yarn. As they made lengths of yarn, weavers rolled them onto the stick so that they would not tangle.

Chavin weavers used the cotton yarn and thread that they spun to make huge burial cloths. They created some of these cloths by weaving and knotting the thread with their fingers. Sometime after 1000 B.C. they began making fabric on large upright looms. These weavers made tapestry, thick fabric with complicated designs woven on the surface with colored threads. They made cloth with the side edges woven so that they would not unravel. They dyed their yarn with vivid colors. Ancient material that they made has a range of more than 200 shades of color. By 400 B.C. Andean weavers had invented every technique that is known to weavers in the world today.

After they established their empire in about A.D. 1000, the Inca developed a factory system for making cloth. Inca rulers gave cotton and wool to weavers, who made it into cloth using backstrap looms. This cloth was used for making army uniforms. The workers also made cloth from

△▽△▽△▽△▽△▽△▽△▽△▽△▽△▽△▽△▽△▽△

ANCIENT CROCHETING
South American needleworkers crocheted gauze fabric that resembled lace by using fine cotton thread and a long needle, rather than a hook like modern crocheters use. Ancient crocheters also used a needle to make netting by knotting and looping cotton thread. The Nazca, whose culture arose in what is now Peru in about 600 B.C., used netting to make items ranging from fishing nets to hairnets.

▽△▽△▽△▽△▽△▽△▽△▽△▽△▽△▽△▽△▽

the fiber that was provided by the government to clothe their families.

The rulers and workers in Inca society wore similar styles of clothing. Men dressed in tunics that came to their knees. On top of their tunics they wore loose capes. Women wore floor-length

▲▽▲▽▲▽▲▽▲▽▲▽▲▽▲▽▲▽▲▽▲▽▲▽

CLOTH OF GOLD

The Inca used a wooden framed loom to make cloth that was reserved for royalty. This was called *cumbi* cloth. Sometimes weavers used gold threads in this fabric. When the Inca conquered another group of people they gave the conquered rulers cumbi cloth. By accepting the gift they officially accepted the Inca as their leaders.

▼▲▽▲▽▲▽▲▽▲▽▲▽▲▽▲▽▲▽▲▽▲▽

tunics with a braided belt wrapped around their waists. The women covered their hair with cloth. In warm climates the Inca people made these garments from thin cotton material. People who lived high in the Andes Mountains, where the weather is cool, wore clothing that they made from llama wool. Even though the styles of clothing were similar for royalty and common people, the quality of cloth that was used to make garments differed. Inca rulers wore clothing made from very fine material that was elaborately decorated. Common people wore garments made from plain, more coarsely woven cloth.

The Mapuche, who lived in what are now Chile and Argentina, wove material to make ponchos. Ponchos are pieces of material that are folded in half and have a hole for the wearer's neck. The sides of ponchos are not sewn. Spaniards copied this style and took it back to Europe. Today ponchos are popular throughout the world.

Weaving and Woven Clothing of Mesoamerica

The earliest cloth that the Maya of Mesoamerica wove on their backstrap looms was made from white and brown cotton. In addition to cotton, the Maya also used agave and yucca fibers to make fabric. Sometimes they wove rabbit fur and feathers into the material that they made. When Maya weavers began dying yarn and cloth, they started weaving material with patterns, including checks and stripes. They made many kinds of fabric, including twill, gauze, and brocade, which is a fabric with a raised design. Their finest fabrics served as gifts and as wrappings for the dead. The Maya traded material to the Aztec as well as other culture groups. According to the Spanish conquistadores, Maya fabric equaled the finest cloth of Europe.

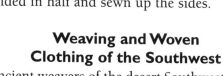

AN OLD TRADITION BECOMES A MODERN STYLE

The brightly colored, patterned fabrics that are produced by the Maya of Guatemala and Chiapas, Mexico, today are sold in stores throughout the world. They are part of a weaving tradition that stretches centuries into the past.

Like the Maya, Aztec weavers also used backstrap looms. The clothing that Maya and Aztec people made from the cloth that they wove was simple in style. In Aztec society ordinary people wore clothing made from agave, or maguey, cloth. Wealthy people and rulers wore clothing made from cotton that was elaborately decorated.

Maya and Aztec men wore loincloths, or breechclouts, made of cloth. They also wore cloaks made from a rectangular piece of cloth. They wrapped the material around themselves under one arm and knotted it over their other shoulder. Women wore ankle-length skirts and belts. They wore tops made from fabric that was folded in half and sewn up the sides.

Weaving and Woven Clothing of the Southwest

Ancient weavers of the desert Southwest began to use finger weaving to make cloth in about 1000 B.C. By A.D. 100 the Hohokam people, who lived in what is now Arizona, were using the backstrap loom to weave cloth from the cotton that they grew. They made this cloth into breechclouts, wraparound skirts, shirts, and head coverings.

In about A.D. 700 the Anasazi people of the Southwest were using agave and yucca fibers to finger-weave sashes, or belts, and ponchos. At first they suspended warp threads from a loop of string, but after they started growing cotton

Pueblo women of the Southwest wore cloth dresses that draped over one shoulder. Pueblo people wove the cloth for these dresses as well as the belts that kept them in place. Before the Spaniards arrived in the Southwest, Pueblo weavers made cloth from cotton. In this photo taken in 1900 the Zuni women's dresses are made of wool. *(National Archives and Records Administration—College Park/Photograph No. NWDNS-79-HPS-6-3274)*

In this 1933 Bureau of Indian Affairs photograph, a Navajo woman from the Ganado district weaves a rug. *(National Archives and Records Administration Pacific Alaska Region/Photograph No. NRIS-75-PAO50-NAVRUG3)*

they began weaving with backstrap looms. The Anasazi weavers also used wooden-framed upright looms to make blankets.

Their descendants, the Pueblo people, continued this tradition. Although women in other culture groups did the weaving, Pueblo weavers were men. Pueblo men wore breechclouts made of cloth and simple cotton shirts. Women of Pueblo tribes wore dresses that had one shoulder.

When the Pueblo people sought refuge among the Dineh (Diné, Navajo) from the Spaniards, the Dineh learned how to weave. They began making cotton blankets and cotton cloth for dresses and shirts. By the 1700s Dineh women began weaving blankets from cotton and from wool they obtained from sheep that the Spaniards had imported. In 1795 Fernando de Chacon, the Spanish governor of New Mexico, praised the weaving of Dineh women, saying they "work their wool with more delicacy and taste than the Spaniards."

Weaving and Woven Clothing of the Northwest

Indian people of the Northwest sewed some garments from cedar bark. Because the climate in their area was mild, their main concern was keeping dry. The women of the Northwest wore skirts that they made from shredded cedar bark. Although men of the Northwest wore buckskin loincloths, they used very little hide for the rest of their clothing. Both men and women of the coast wore rain capes that women wove. They did not use looms for this. Indian people who lived further inland used cattail leaves to make their rain capes.

The people of the Northwest did weave blankets on looms. The Tsimshian tribe of the Northwest Coast in what is now British Columbia, Canada, made Chilkat blankets on upright looms. They created bold fabrics with geometric patterns and long fringe. To make them, weavers used shredded cedar bark for the warp threads and mountain goat fur for the weft threads. Each blanket took a year to make. Tribal leaders wore these blankets at ceremonies.

Although women spun the yarn and wove the blankets, men made the looms and provided the goatskins with fur on them. Men also made the abstract designs for the blankets. They drew figures, such as eagles and bears, on pattern boards. The technique of making these blankets spread to the Tlingit through trade and marriage.

Salish weavers, who also lived on the northwest coast, used goat, cattail fluff, and fur from their special white dogs to make white blankets. They also made blankets with crossing stripes of darker wool to form plaid designs.

Weaving of the Northeast

Before contact with Europeans, northeastern weavers used finger weaving to produce headbands, belts, sashes, and bags for small objects. They also invented a way to weave shell beads together. These shell beads were called *wampum*. To make woven wampum belts, necklaces, and bracelets they used a bow loom. They made this loom by stringing warp threads through grooved spreader bars. They tied the ends of the strings to the ends of a stick. The tight warp threads made the stick bend like a bow. This technique is still used today for loom beadwork, an art form practiced by people of many North American Indian tribes today.

TIME LINE

6000 to 5000 B.C.	South American Indians begin weaving wild cotton.
4000 B.C.	Indians of the Andes domesticate alpacas.
2000 B.C.	Indians of the Andes begin weaving with looms.
1500 B.C.	Hohokam Indians of the North American Southwest begin growing cotton.
A.D. 1050 to 1300	Anasazi weavers began using a vertical blanket loom to weave intricate blankets of cotton.

7 Wearable Art

Whether they made their clothing from hides or fiber, American Indians added many artistic decorations to the clothing that they wore. They used paints and dyes in order to make their clothing colorful. Some embroidered designs on their clothing. Others sewed shells and colored porcupine quills onto their garments. Throughout the Americas, Indians designed and wore jewelry. In Mesoamerica and South America those who were part of the ruling classes wore jewelry that was made from precious metals and stones.

DYES

American Indians developed the skill to dye both fabric and leather in a number of colors. To make dyes, they used the natural coloring matter, or pigment, from plants and from minerals that they found in the soil. The pigments that they used depended on what was available where they lived. For example, Indians of the Northeast used cranberries as red dye because cranberries grew wild in what is now New England. Indians of Mesoamerica discovered that they could make red dye from tiny insects that lived on a certain type of cactus that was native to the region where they lived.

American Indians used dyes for a number of purposes. The Indians of North America who wore hide clothing painted designs on these garments. In the Northeast, Indians dyed the grasses and fur that they used to embroider designs on garments. Indians of the Northeast and Plains dyed porcupine quills to decorate their clothing. Pueblo people of the Southwest dyed the yucca fibers that they used to make sandals. American Indians who wore little

▲▽▲▽▲▽▲▽▲▽▲▽▲▽▲▽▲▽▲▽▲▽▲▽▲▽▲▽▲▽▲

THE SCIENCE OF DYEING

A dye is a stain. Indians mixed plants and earth that contained pigments with water and then boiled the mixture. This dissolved the pigments so that they would soak into cloth or hide and stain them.

When people spill cranberry or grape juice on their clothing, they wash it. Even though the stain may not come out, it becomes lighter. Indians needed to find a way to keep the color of the stains that they made with dye from fading. In order to fix colors they used mordants. A mordant is a substance that chemically binds with the dye and with the hide or cloth. Good mordants bind the two together without making the fabric or hide stiff.

Indians used wild plum bark, prairie dock roots, and ground cedar as mordants. In the Southwest Indians set dyes with ashes that they boiled in water. Oglala Lakota people collected fine soil that contained alum, a metal salt. They mixed it with ground plants that contained pigment. Then they shaped it into balls and burned it in a fire. When they wanted to dye clothing, they crushed one of these dye-and-mordant balls and mixed it with water.

▽▲▽▲▽▲▽▲▽▲▽▲▽▲▽▲▽▲▽▲▽▲▽▲▽▲▽▲▽▲▽

clothing because they lived in warm climates sometimes painted their skins.

Dyes of the Northeast

In addition to using cranberry juice as dye, Indians of the Northeast obtained red from wild strawberries. They made blue dye from larkspur flowers and blueberries. The Potawatomi used the inner bark from speckled alder and red oak trees for yellow, red, and brown. Bloodroot produced orange, and yellow came from the sap of the spotted touch-me-not and from black-eyed-Susan flowers.

Dyes of the Great Plains

On the plains, the Dakota, Lakota, and Nakota used buffalo berries and chokecherries to produce red dyes. They made yellow from sunflowers and yellow coneflowers.

Dyes of the Northwest and Plateau

In the Northwest and Plateau regions Indians used the roots of the Oregon grape to make a yellow dye. Plateau Indians made dyes from red, orange, and yellow clay, as well as from algae scraped from river rocks that produced a green color.

Dyes of the Southwest

American Indians of the Southwest used more than 20 different kinds of plants to dye fabric. Mountain-mahogany roots produced red dyes; rabbit brush flowers and the entire Indian tea plant yielded yellows. They mixed three-leaf-sumac twigs and leaves with piñon gum to make a deep black color. The Dineh (Navajo) used wild rhubarb roots to produce colors ranging from yellow, orange, and red, to green and brown.

Dyes of Mesoamerica and South America

The Maya, Aztec, and Inca all obtained dye from cochineal, a tiny scale insect. They gathered these insects from prickly pear cacti that they had planted to serve as a home to the insects. Then they killed the insects in boiling water and dried them in the sun until they turned a silver color. Finally they ground the insects into powder. A substance in the body of the insects produced reds as well as shades of orange, pink, and purple for fabric.

Indians of Mesoamerica and the Circum-Caribbean made blue dye from the indigo plant. They discovered how to remove a yellow substance, indoxyl, from the plants. To do this, first they soaked the plants in water and then let them

▲▽▲▽▲▽▲▽▲▽▲▽▲▽▲▽▲▽▲▽▲▽▲▽▲▽▲

COCHINEAL TRADE

When Spanish conquistador Hernán Cortés and his men arrived in the Americas, they saw brilliant red cotton cloth and rabbit fur yarn being sold in the marketplaces of the Aztec cities. They were impressed by the quality of the color. Although Europeans knew how to make red dyes, the pigments they had used were expensive and difficult to obtain. Immediately the Spaniards knew they had found a way to make money. Soon cochineal became the most widely traded and most valuable product of the West Indies after gold and silver. In England the dye was used to produce the red coats that were part of the military uniform. (British soldiers were called "redcoats.") Today cochineal is a luxury dye for weavers and fabric artists. It is also still used by Mexican rug weavers in certain areas. The red dye is also used in cosmetics and for artists' pigments.

▽▲▽▲▽▲▽▲▽▲▽▲▽▲▽▲▽▲▽▲▽▲▽▲▽▲▽

set for 10 to 15 hours. When a yellow liquid had formed, they stirred it until it combined with oxygen in the air and turned bright blue. Later, European colonists established large indigo plantations in North and South Carolina and in Georgia with indigo plant seeds that they had obtained in the West Indies.

Maya dyers obtained purple coloring for their fabric from shellfish, or mollusks, called murex that they gathered from the seacoast. They rubbed the murexes against each other to extract the pigment from a gland in the shellfish.

South American and Mesoamerican dyers invented special methods to color material or yarn so that it had patterns. The Maya painted intricate designs on fabric. Experts who study the Maya culture believe that Maya weavers may also have painted on material with wax and then dipped the material in dye. The wax kept the dye from coloring the places it covered. Once they had dyed the material, they heated it to remove the wax. Maya weavers printed some of their fabrics with pottery stamps and cylinders that they dipped in dye.

Sometimes Maya weavers tied tight bands around hanks or skeins of cotton yarn. The tied places did not soak up dye. They measured the yarn and carefully spaced the ties. When weavers used yarn that they had colored in this way, it made patterns in the cloth that they made. This method of dying yarn is called ikat. Weavers who lived in what is now Chile also used this technique.

▲▽▲▽▲▽▲▽▲▽▲▽▲▽▲▽▲▽▲▽▲▽▲▽▲▽▲

TIE-DYEING

The Moche, who lived in what is now Peru between 200 B.C. and A.D. 600 made beautiful patterns in fabric they had woven by tie-dying it. In order to tie-dye fabric, they sometimes sewed tiny puckers or pleats in loosely woven, light cloth with a needle and thread. Other times they stitched small circles or squares with their thread and pulled it tightly. When they had finished sewing, they dipped the cloth in a dye bath. Because the puckers were bunched together, they did not absorb as much dye as the rest of the material so that they were a lighter color. Once the cloth had been dyed, they removed the stitches.

▽▲▽▲▽▲▽▲▽▲▽▲▽▲▽▲▽▲▽▲▽▲▽▲▽▲▽

EMBROIDERY

American Indians also decorated clothing by sewing designs onto fabric with colored thread. This is called embroidery. Indians of many North American tribes embroidered their clothing. American

The Maya were known for the fine cotton cloth that they wove and for their skill at embroidery. This photograph of a young Maya woman was taken at the Temple of Jaguars in Chichén Itzá in the 1920s. *(Latin American Library, Tulane University, Ernest Crandall Collection)*

Indians of the Northeast dyed moose hair to use as embroidery thread to make floral designs. Some tribes in North America used dyed plant fibers as embroidery thread.

In Mesoamerica, the Maya are best known for their skill as embroiderers. Maya needleworkers sewed the cloth they wanted to decorate onto a wooden frame or the top of a round basket. This served as an embroidery hoop. Then they sketched the design on the cloth with a bird quill dipped in indigo dye. Using threads that they had dyed bright colors, they filled the design with stitches.

The Nazca of what is now Peru were expert embroiderers by about 400 B.C. They used decorative stitches to create borders for huge cloths. These embroiderers used the stem stitch, a flat stitch, to produce their designs. Fine examples of Nazca embroidery and textiles exist today because the dry climate of Peru's southern coast has preserved them.

Nazca embroiderers also used a long metal needle to make a kind of knitted

▲▽▲▽▲▽▲▽▲▽▲▽▲▽▲▽▲▽▲▽▲▽▲▽▲▽▲

BELLS AND SHELLS

In addition to using threads, Indians of Mesoamerica decorated their clothing by sewing metal bells that they had made onto the fabric. Sometimes they drilled tiny holes in shells and sewed them onto fabric as well. Many Indians of North America decorated their clothing with shells that they obtained from other Indians in trade. In some instances, the shells came from many hundreds of miles away.

▼▲▼▲▼▲▼▲▼▲▼▲▼▲▼▲▼▲▼▲▼▲▼▲▼▲▼

edging for pieces of material. This three-dimensional embroidery sometimes portrayed tiny people, less than an inch tall. These people were made from thread spun from alpaca or llama wool. They had detailed facial features and costumes. Usually they were shown carrying staffs or fans. Other decorative borders that Nazca embroiderers made portrayed birds and other animals and abstract designs.

QUILLWORK

In addition to embroidery, North American Indians decorated clothing and other items by sewing dyed porcupine quills to them with sinew. They are the only people in the world known to do quillwork. Indians of the Plains were experts at this art. Indians of the Northeast, especially those who lived in the Great Lakes area, were also known for their quillwork.

To obtain quills, American Indians carefully pulled them from porcupines that they had hunted. Hard and sharp, the quills serve as a porcupine's defense against other animals. Next the Indians cleaned the quills and sorted them according to size. After that, quill workers boiled them in a mixture of water and plant materials to dye them. Once again they let the quills dry and then they cut off the sharp tips.

When they were ready to use the quills, Indians softened them in their mouths and flattened them by pulling them between their teeth. They sewed long stitches on leather with sinew, the tough fiber that holds an animal's muscles to its bones. Then they folded the flattened quills around these sinew stitches in order to make designs. Indians of North America often decorated the insteps and tongues of their moccasins as well as their leather clothing with quill embroidery. Sometimes they wove the flattened quills on a bow loom to create patterned belts.

After contact with Europeans, American Indians began decorating clothing with the glass beads and silk thread that Europeans had

In addition to using porcupine quills as a decoration, Plains Indians used the long guard hairs that surround the quills. Men of many Plains tribes wore porcupine hair roaches such as the one worn by this young Cree man from Saskatchewan in 1903. *(G. E. Fleming, Photographer/ National Archives of Canada/Photograph No. PA-028983)*

brought to trade. They adapted their quillwork designs to beadwork. By the 1800s beadwork had nearly replaced quillwork.

FEATHERWORK

American Indians used feathers to decorate their clothing. They also made accessories from feathers, such as hats, headdresses, and fans. Many tribes had professional hunters who were responsible for obtaining the feathers they needed for these projects. Often they traded for feathers from faraway places. When they could not obtain feathers that were the color they wanted, ancient feather workers used dyes to paint feathers. They attached feathers to clothing and leather by gluing, sewing, or tying them.

In North America, Indians of some tribes skinned birds and sewed the hides together to make clothing. One of the oldest feathered garments found in North America is a cape from Nevada that has been dated to 2500 B.C. The Inuit skinned seabirds, such as cormorants and puffins, and used them for making parkas. The birds' feathers served as insulation against the cold. Indians of the Southeast made capes from feathered bird skins.

In addition to using the whole skin of birds, Indians of the Arctic and the Northwest cut spiral strips from bird skins with the feathers left on them. They wove these strips into capes. Indians of the Southeast and Southern Plains tied individual feathers onto netting in order to make capes.

Indians of North America used individual feathers in a variety of ways as well. Male Plains Indians tied eagle feathers to their hair and on fringes of their clothing. They used eagle feathers for their headdresses as well. Plains Indians made fans of eagle tail feathers and wing feathers. Members of different North American tribes made a number of very different styles of headdresses from feathers.

The Olmec were the first Mesoamerican Indians to do featherwork. They used feathers to make headdresses. The Maya also practiced the craft of featherworking. They made capes, stoles, tassels, belts, earrings, shields, and fans, both for cooling themselves and for fanning the flames of

The Aztec attached feathers to clothing. Sometimes they wove feathers into material. The men wearing feather suits in this detail from a drawing made in 1525 were Aztec soldiers. *(Library of Congress, Prints and Photographs Division [LC-USZ62-124461])*

▲▽▲▽▲▽▲▽▲▽▲▽▲▽▲▽▲▽▲▽▲▽▲▽▲▽▲▽

FAVORITE FEATHERS

Mesoamerican and South American featherworkers preferred to work with parrot, macaw, hummingbird, and quetzal feathers. They prized quetzal feathers the most because of their brilliant and iridescent green color.

▽▲▽▲▽▲▽▲▽▲▽▲▽▲▽▲▽▲▽▲▽▲▽▲▽▲▽▲▽

fires. The Aztec, whose empire was established in Mexico in about A.D. 1100, made similar items from feathers.

Both Maya and Aztec featherworkers made brilliant cloth from feathers. They spun the feathers into the yarn they used for weft threads, the crosswise threads in a fabric. The featherwork of Mesoamerica is so delicate that today the career of a featherworker is over by the time a person reaches the age of 50 because of the toll the work takes on the eyes.

JEWELRY

From the earliest times Indians throughout the Americas made jewelry from shells, stones, and metal. Both men and women wore jewelry, including rings, earrings, and pendants. Indian people also made beads that they strung into necklaces.

Often they used shells to make beads. Sometimes they cut off the ends of certain types of shells to make hollow cylinders that they could string together for necklaces. In other instances, they drilled holes in shells with a stone drill in order to string them. They polished shells by rubbing them with sand. American Indians of the western part of what is now the United States used large

This photo of young Indian men who lived in southwestern Idaho in 1897 shows how Plains and Plateau Indians combined feathers, shells, and fringe to decorate their clothing. The long white beads that make up their breastplates are made from bone. Before contact with Europeans, Indians used porcupine quills instead of glass beads and buttons. *(National Archives and Records Administration—College Park/Photograph No. NWDNS-75-SEI-20)*

circles cut from abalone shells as pendants. These shells that were found off the Pacific coast of what is now California were traded as far as the Great Plains.

The semiprecious stones that Indians used for their jewelry included opal, topaz, agate, and turquoise. The Hohokam and Anasazi people of the Southwest mined turquoise, a blue-green stone, in what are now Arizona and New Mexico. Indian miners began digging turquoise in about 200 B.C. to provide gemstones for beads and mosaic inlays. Indian artisans also carved turquoise. They traded the stones with the Aztec of Mesoamerica. The Aztec believed that the turquoise stones contained fire and had the ability to heal. They made rings, necklaces, lip plugs, masks, and chest ornaments from turquoise, often setting the stone into gold.

The Olmec and Maya of Mesoamerica used jade, a green stone, for jewelry. Olmec jadeworkers were so skilled at working with this hard gemstone that they made paper-thin ear ornaments. They cut the pieces of jade with a saw made from a cotton string or a strip of leather. They coated the string with wet sand or crushed jade that served as an abrasive. Then they polished the stone with sand or crushed jade to make it shiny. The Aztec used jade for jewelry too. Olmec and Maya jadeworkers also made ornaments for clothing. They sewed them onto the fabric, sometimes in combination with feathers and gold.

The first Indians to make metal jewelry in the Americas were Paleo-Indians who lived in the Great Lakes region of North America. Beginning in about 5000 to 4000 B.C., they made beads, rings, pendants,

SILVER AND TURQUOISE
A New Southwest Tradition

A Dineh (Navajo) man named Atsidi Sani is credited with becoming the first silversmith. In the mid-1800s a Mexican blacksmith taught him to work with iron. Afterward he taught himself and his sons how to work with silver. They taught others. At first Dineh silversmiths made bells from quarters. They also made small tobacco cases and silver bridles for horses. Later Dineh silversmiths learned how to cast silver in molds from Mexicans as well. It is very likely that some of these teachers were descendants of the Aztec.

Atsidi Chom was the first Dineh silversmith to set turquoise into silver in a ring that he made in the late 1870s. Soon he began making more rings and began creating bracelets. Young men who watched him started making jewelry in the style he had created. The Zuni and Hopi began making silver jewelry too. Southwestern silver jewelry set with turquoise stones is popular throughout the world today.

bracelets, and breast-plates from copper. They hammered the copper into thin sheets and bent it to make this jewelry. These Paleo-Indians are thought to be the first metalworkers in the world, so the jewelry they produced perhaps was the first of its kind.

▲▼▲▼▲▼▲▼▲▼▲▼▲▼▲▼▲▼▲▼▲▼▲▼▲

HOW JADE WAS NAMED

The word *jade* originated with the Spaniards. When the conquistadores first saw the green mineral in the Americas, they called it *piedra de hijada,* meaning "stone of the kidneys." They chose the name because they thought these green stones could heal kidney problems. Later *hijada,* or kidney, was abbreviated to jade.

▼▲▼▲▼▲▼▲▼▲▼▲▼▲▼▲▼▲▼▲▼▲▼▲▼

Indians of Mesoamerica and South America used gold for much of their jewelry. They also used some silver. Beginning about 4,000 years ago, metalworkers in what is now Ecuador began making jewelry from gold and copper. By about 1,000 years ago, metalworkers in what is now Mexico were making beautiful gold jewelry. The Inca of South America also made jewelry from gold.

In the late 1500s the Spanish conquistadores melted down most of the jewelry that the Aztec and the Inca made. Many of the ingots, or gold and silver bars, that they shipped were formed from jewelry that they had melted down. In 1492 about $200 million worth of gold and silver existed in Europe, either hidden away or exchanged as money. By 1600 that amount of gold and silver had increased by eight times because of all the precious metals the conquistadores shipped home to Europe.

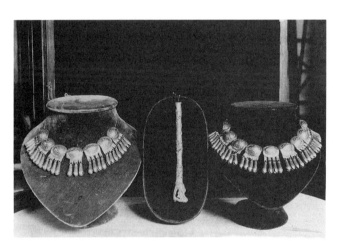

Mesoamerican goldsmiths created intricate jewelry and other objects. These creations were reserved for Aztec rulers. The wand in the center of this picture would have been carried by a person of authority in Aztec government or a priest. *(Library of Congress, Prints and Photographs Division [LC-USZ62-112914])*

8

Baskets and Pottery

American Indians of many culture groups wove baskets from fibers. They made some of them for storing their food. They made other baskets to use when they prepared food. These included strainers and waterproof bowls, cups, and cooking baskets. They also made pottery bowls and jars for food storage and cooking. Pottery is made from clay that is heated so that it hardens. Clay is made up of fine pieces of soil that have been carried by rivers and streams and deposited in lakes or ponds.

BASKETS

Archaeologists, scientists who study the past, believe that as early as 8000 B.C. American Indians of the North American Great Basin made tightly woven twine baskets in which they cooked food. Indian people cooked food by putting it into a basket and adding water. Then they heated the water by dropping hot rocks into it.

Some tribes used basketweaving methods for making hats. Many Indians who lived in warm climates wore sandals that were woven from sturdy fibers. The Aleut people of the Arctic used long, thin strands of grass to weave socks in the same way that they wove their baskets. Babies of some tribes slept in baby carriers that were specially woven baskets.

Indians made their baskets from fibers of plants that were common where they lived. They often dyed these fibers bright colors with juices from plants that they had gathered. They wove the colored fibers into intricate patterns. Sometimes they decorated their baskets with feathers or shells. Some basket makers made designs on their baskets with embroidery.

American Indians used many methods to make baskets. Two of these were more common than others. The first was a coiled basket.

▲▽▲▽▲▽▲▽▲▽▲▽▲▽▲▽▲▽▲▽▲▽▲▽▲▽▲

BASKETS OF MESOAMERICA AND SOUTH AMERICA

Indian people of Mesoamerica and South America were making baskets long before the Europeans arrived on their shores. Not much is known about their baskets because European writers and collectors focused on their pottery, jewelry, and fabrics. Basket making traditions began to die out among many groups of Mesoamerican and South American Indians after they were colonized. Only recently have collectors begun to be interested in the baskets still being made by some groups of Indians in these areas.

▽▲▽▲▽▲▽▲▽▲▽▲▽▲▽▲▽▲▽▲▽▲▽▲▽▲▽

To make a coiled basket, a basket maker twisted or braided plant fibers into long ropes after soaking them in water to soften them. To shape a coiled basket, the basket maker coiled a rope into a spiral to make a flat bottom, sewing the coils together with a bone needle as she or he worked. The most finely made coiled baskets contain thousands of individual stitches. When they had finished a flat base, basket makers then laid coils on top of one another so that they formed the sides of the basket. They made patterns on these baskets by wrapping the coils with colored fibers.

American Indians found many uses for the baskets that they made. The Pomo, a California tribe, wove these coiled baskets. They used them to prepare mush and bread made from acorns. *(Survey Report of Fresno and Madera counties by L.D. Creel ca. 1920/National Archives and Records Administration Pacific Region/ Photograph No. NRHS-75-SAO-CODED-150FRESNO-16)*

The second kind of basket was made by using an over-and-under style of weaving that is called wickerwork or checkerwork. To make these baskets, Indians first made hoops from sturdy material such as bark or willow twigs. These hoops helped the basket keep its shape. Then the basket maker wove fibers together in an over-and-under pattern, like that used to make cloth, to connect the parts of the basket frame. Because baskets needed to be strong, basket makers sometimes twisted or braided several fibers to make thicker strands to use in their weaving. They made bags from twined or braided fibers in addition to baskets.

Baskets of the Northeast and Southeast

Indians of the Northeast and Southeast made baskets from many types of plants. Some of their favorite materials included sweetgrass, cattails, bulrushes, and dogbane. Indians of the Southeast often used long pine needles for many of their coiled baskets. They decorated their baskets with floral and animal designs with fibers that they had dyed. Some of the plants that they used for dyes were black walnut, cranberries, and blueberries.

In the 1600s Indians of the Northeast, in the area that is now called New England, including the Penobscot and Nipmuc, began making woven splint baskets from ash and oak trees. A splint is a long, thin piece of wood. Men would harvest the trees and cut them into logs that were a little taller than a person. Then they pounded on a log with a hammer to make the wood fibers split from the log along the tree rings that marked each year's growth. They shaved splints from these thin pieces of wood with a curved knife. The earliest knives were made from beaver incisor teeth. In the 1700s and 1800s Indians of the Northeast began selling splint baskets to their white neighbors who used them for sewing baskets.

American Indians passed the knowledge of how to make baskets from elders to youngsters. This Cherokee basket weaver, who is making a wickerwork basket, lived in North Carolina. *(National Archives and Records Administration Southeast Region/Photograph No. NRCA-435-ART001-EN334A[1])*

Baskets of the Arctic

The Aleut people who live on the coast and islands of what is now Alaska made baskets from many materials, including spruce roots and beach grass, that grew in the summer. Archaeologists have found pieces of baskets that these people made about 500 years ago. Basket makers gathered grass in summer. They bleached it to turn it a light tan color by soaking it in saltwater and leaving it in the sun to dry. The baskets they made were so tightly woven that they were waterproof.

Basket makers of the Arctic dyed the grass with berries that they gathered during the short summer season, including black-berries, and with crushed flowers or bark. They mixed seal oil and charcoal to make black dye.

▲▽▲▽▲▽▲▽▲▽▲▽▲▽▲▽▲▽▲▽▲▽▲▽▲▽▲

MITTENS AND SOCKS

Aleut basket makers wove mittens and socks from beach grass. Some historians believe that in addition to keeping wearers warm, the socks and mittens kept the wearers' hands and feet dry.

▽▲▽▲▽▲▽▲▽▲▽▲▽▲▽▲▽▲▽▲▽▲▽▲▽▲▽

When they had finished weaving their baskets, they decorated them by embroidering the baskets with strands of maidenhair fern. Often they used feathers on their baskets. Sometimes they edged the baskets around the top with strands of animal intestines that they had dyed.

Baskets of the Northwest

Basket makers of the Northwest Coast wove containers from cedar bark and beach grass. The Tlingit, Haida, Tsimshian, and Bella Coola were known for their skill at basket weaving. Although they made wooden boxes for cooking and storing some foods, they used baskets to prepare and store other foods.

Basket artisans of the Northwest devised hundreds of patterns for their baskets. Some of these designs were figures of whales, fish, birds, and insects. Some tribes wove whaling scenes into their bas-ketwork. Different tribes made baskets that had unique designs.

▲▽▲▽▲▽▲▽▲▽▲▽▲▽▲▽▲▽▲▽▲▽▲▽▲▽▲

WOVEN HATS

American Indian basket weavers of the Northwest Coast made wide-brimmed rain hats from spruce root. The oldest Northwest Coast rain hat was found in what is now Tacoma, Washington. Since it was found near a fishing weir, or trap, it probably belonged to a fisher. Archaeologists believe that it is between 400 and 1,000 years old.

The Haida were especially known for their skill at hat making. They painted plain hats after they had been woven. They traded hats with neighboring tribes for items that they needed.

▽▲▽▲▽▲▽▲▽▲▽▲▽▲▽▲▽▲▽▲▽▲▽▲▽

Baskets of California

Southern California tribes, including the Pomo, Maidu, and Hupa made coiled baskets from willow, rushes, and a tall white grass that is called sedge grass.

Indians who lived in what is now California waterproofed baskets by coating them inside and on the outside with asphalt, a sticky petroleum substance. They coated the insides of bottles with narrow necks by heating the asphalt and pouring some into the basket. Then they put pebbles inside the basket and shook it. The movement of the pebbles evenly distributed the asphalt on the inside surface of the basket. They used these baskets for carrying and storing water and other liquids.

▲▽▲▽▲▽▲▽▲▽▲▽▲▽▲▽▲▽▲▽▲▽▲▽▲▽▲

DYEING FIBERS

Pomo basket makers dyed bulrushes brown or black by burying them in wet ashes. Indians of other tribes buried fibers that they used for basket making so that they would absorb mineral pigments from the earth.

▽▲▽▲▽▲▽▲▽▲▽▲▽▲▽▲▽▲▽▲▽▲▽▲▽▲▽

The Pomo people were known for their basket weaving craftsmanship. They wove feathers, down, and shells into their designs. As a challenge of their skill, some Pomo weavers wove baskets the size of the head of a pin. Unlike the other North American tribes in which women were responsible for making baskets, in the Pomo tribe both women and men made baskets.

Baskets of the Plateau and Great Basin

Plateau and Great Basin basket weavers are known for their tall, round baskets and for flat baskets that they made from hemp, a plant with sturdy fibers. Indians of the Plateau embroidered their baskets with colored grasses.

The Paiute Indians of the Great Basin made baskets that they carried with them when they gathered seeds. They also made specially shaped winnowing baskets that they used to toss seeds into the air and catch them. This tossing and catching loosened the seed husks, or coatings. In addition to winnowing baskets, Paiute basket makers wove canteens from fiber to carry water. These bottle-shaped baskets had straps to make them more practical. Paiute basket makers waterproofed them by coating them with pitch, the sticky sap from trees.

Baskets of the Southwest

Some of the oldest pieces of basket fragments in North America have been found in the Southwest, where the dry climate has preserved them. Some of them are more than 10,000 years old. An ancient Southwest group of people who are called the Basket Makers today wove storage and cooking baskets as well as sandals from yucca fibers. They made baskets by coiling them and by weaving horizontal and vertical fibers. The Basket Makers lived from about 100 B.C. to A.D. 700. Later the Hopi, Akimel O'odham (Pima), Ute, and Apache Indians all made baskets. Like the Paiute, the Apache made waterproof baskets. They used piñon pitch to coat them.

In the early 1900s non-Indians in the United States began collecting American Indian baskets to display in their homes. Indians started making baskets for the tourists as a source of income. Soon non-Indian manufacturers began imitating the traditional Indian designs. Many of the baskets sold in home decorating stores today are based on traditional designs that Indian basket makers created hundreds of years ago. Today baskets made by enrolled members of Indian tribes are popular with art collectors.

POTTERY

From making coiled baskets, Indian people learned skills that they would later use to shape jars and bowls from clay. The oldest piece of pottery in the Americas was discovered in the Amazon Basin of South America and is between 7,000 and 8,000 years old. The second oldest pottery was found in what is now Colombia in South America. It was dated at 3000 B.C. In addition to bowls and jars, Indian potters of the Americas eventually began making plates, boxes, incense burners, and palettes for mixing paint. They also made figurines, or little pottery statues. Some of these were hollow and others were solid.

To shape their pottery, American Indian potters used three methods: coiling, molding, and modeling. They made coiled pots by placing long, thin clay cylinders in a spiral to form a base and walls. After they had done this, they smoothed them. They made molded pottery objects by pressing damp clay into a form, or mold, so that the clay took its shape. Indian potters

Anasazi potters, who lived in what is now the "four corners" area of the Southwest, created drinking vessels remarkably similar to modern coffee mugs in design. *(U.S. Bureau of Ethnography)*

also used their fingers and sculpting tools to shape and carve pottery objects.

Pottery of South America

The first potters of the Amazon Basin made shallow bowls and cooking pots that they used to boil food. They decorated their pots with strips of clay that they applied to the surface of the container. Pottery making spread to what is now Peru about 1,000 years later. There Chavin potters began firing their pottery in kilns, or ovens, that were lined with clay. Chavin culture arose in about 1500 B.C. The kilns that Chavin potters constructed helped them to control the temperature of the pots they were firing.

The Moche, whose culture flourished in what is now Peru from about 200 B.C. to about A.D. 800, were perhaps the finest potters in the world. Their best-known creations were life-sized and lifelike portraits of people's faces. The Moche transformed the craft of pottery into an art form by making molded pottery vessels that reflected the world around them. In doing so, they left a historical record of their lives in clay. Some of the Moche jars resemble agricultural products, including potatoes, beans, peanuts, cotton, fruit, and cacao. Moche potters also painted scenes on the sides of smooth-sided jars. They created musical jars in the shape of birds. These were designed so that when water was poured out, it forced air through a whistle.

Pottery of Mesoamerica

The first Indian potters of Mesoamerica began working in about 2000 B.C. When they had finished shaping the pots, they covered them with a coating of thin clay called a slip. The most popular colors for this finish coating were black, brown, red, and white. To smooth the surface of their pots, they rubbed them with a smooth pebble. They made designs on pots by carving them into the surface with a sharp stick. They also painted designs on some pots with hot wax. When they dipped these pots into pigments, the wax resisted the color. Later they removed the wax.

Beginning in about A.D. 300, Teotihuacán potters began making figurines in the shape of people. The Teotihuacán culture arose in the Valley of Mexico in about 150 B.C. and lasted to about A.D. 650. These images had legs and arms that could move. Potters decorated their pots and jars with dark brown or black slip and then scratched

▲▽▲▽▲▽▲▽▲▽▲▽▲▽▲▽▲▽▲▽▲▽▲▽▲▽▲▽▲

MUSICAL INSTRUMENTS FROM CLAY

Ancient people of the Americas made musical instruments from fired clay. The oldest instruments were whistles. The earliest clay whistle found so far is 1,500 years old and was made by the Maya of Mesoamerica. (Maya culture arose in about 1500 B.C.) Other instruments that American Indian potters created included flutes, drums, and horns.

▽▲▽▲▽▲▽▲▽▲▽▲▽▲▽▲▽▲▽▲▽▲▽▲▽▲▽▲▽

designs into them. Sometimes they painted these designs with cinnabar, a red mineral that is a form of mercury.

The Maya, who inhabited the Yucatán Peninsula of what is now Mexico at this time, also made figurines in the shape of people. Maya figurines had clothing that could be removed. One of the most unique pottery items the Maya made was a jar with a locking, twist-off lid in about A.D. 400. These flat-bottomed jars were large enough to hold about a gallon of liquid.

In about A.D. 900 Maya potters began using pigments to color their pots. These produced a more decorative effect, but had to be fired at a lower temperature than plain pots did, so that the items they made were more fragile. They also developed paint rollers and stamps in order to decorate their clay vessels.

The Aztec, who established an empire in what is now Mexico in about A.D. 1100, made pottery as well. They sold their pots in the marketplaces of large cities. Bernard Díaz del Castillo, a Spaniard who recorded Aztec life shortly after the arrival of Cortez, wrote that he saw ". . . every sort of pottery, made in a thousand forms from great water jars to little jugs" at the market in Tlatelolco near what would eventually become Mexico City.

Pottery of North America

In North America potters of the Northeast, Southeast, and Southwest made bowls and pots. Often early potters used gray or blue-gray clay. They pressed objects such as a corncob or a roughly woven piece of cloth into the wet clay to produce an interesting texture.

In the Northeast and Southeast, Indians began making pottery about 5,000 years ago. To form their pots, they pinched the clay into

▲▼▲▼▲▼▲▼▲▼▲▼▲▼▲▼▲▼▲▼▲▼▲▼▲▼▲

ADDING TEMPER TO CLAY

In order to thicken clay so that it is easier to work with, potters add substances that are called temper to it. Temper also keeps the clay from shrinking and cracking when it is fired. Potters of the Northeast and Southeast used crushed bone, shells and potsherds (pieces of broken pots) for temper. They also used sand and cattail or milkweed fluff. Potters of the Southwest used crushed volcanic rock. They also used potsherds, sand, quartz, and mica. Because mica reflects light, it made the surface of the pots sparkle.

▼▲▼▲▼▲▼▲▼▲▼▲▼▲▼▲▼▲▼▲▼▲▼▲▼▲▼

the shape they wanted. They fired the pots in shallow pits. In addition to making pots, they also made clay pipes for smoking tobacco.

Southwestern potters began by making gray clay cooking vessels. Later they began working with pink or red clay and making pitchers and mugs. They used vegetable dyes to paint geometric designs on many of the items that they made. The Anasazi, whose culture arose in the Southwest in about 350 B.C., produced a great deal of pottery. So did the Fremont people, who lived in the eastern Great Basin from A.D. 400 to A.D. 1300.

Pueblo potters, the descendants of the Anasazi, began using finer clay for their pots than their ancestors had used. They also discovered that if they controlled the amount of oxygen from the air that contacted their pots when they were firing them, then they could change the color of the finished pots. To keep oxygen from getting to the pots, they covered them with ashes when they fired them. After European contact they used powdered cow dung. This produced black pots from red clay.

The pots on the floor of this Acoma Pueblo home are in different stages of completion. The three pots on the left are raw clay. The pot in the center has been painted. The two pots on the right have been fired to harden them. This picture was taken in 1900. *(National Archives and Records Administration—College Park/Photograph No. NWDNS-79-HPS-6-1563)*

They made shiny surfaces on pots by using colored slips to give their pots a smoother finish. After the pot had been fired, the Pueblo potter rubbed it with a stone to polish it. Southwestern potters incised, or cut, designs onto their bowls and jars with sharp sticks, and they painted designs on them with vegetable dyes. Often they made geometric designs. Some potters made pictures of birds, animals, and insects. Today the Pueblo people of the Southwest continue to produce pottery. Each pueblo is known for its distinctive pottery designs. These pots have become collectors' items.

COOL WATER IN THE HOT DESERT

Because potters of the Southwest did not use hard glazes to cover the surface of their pots, they were not completely waterproof. This was a good thing in the hot desert climate. When Indians stored water in pottery jars, it slowly seeped to the outside surface of the pot, where it evaporated. This lowered the temperature of the water inside the jar.

TIME LINE	
8000 B.C.	Indians of the Great Basin and Southwest make baskets.
6000 B.C. to 5000 B.C.	Indians of the Amazon Basin begin making pottery.
2700 B.C.	Indians of the Southeast make pottery.
1000 B.C.	Indians along the entire Atlantic coast of North America are making pottery.
900 B.C.	Chavin potters, who live in what is now Peru, invent the refractory kiln.
200 B.C. to A.D. 800	Moche potters in what is now Peru shape pottery objects that some modern art historians believe are the finest in the world.
A.D. 400	Maya potters invent a locking, twist-off jar lid.
A.D. 700 to A.D. 1100	Pueblo Indians of the Southwest make shiny-surfaced pots. They begin to create the shapes and designs that are still made and collected today.

9

Painting and Sculpture

 The very first American Indian artists made cave paintings throughout the Americas, using mineral pigments for paint. These earliest Indian artists also chipped pictures and designs into rocks. These are called petroglyphs. (*Petro* means rock, and a *glyph* is a symbol.)

For thousands of years art continued to be important to American Indian people. It provided them with a way to record their history. Their art was also a way to express their spiritual beliefs. Finally, the artworks that they created added beauty to their surroundings.

North American Indians of the Great Plains painted on hides. Mesoamerican Indians, including the Maya and Aztec, painted large pictures, or murals, on their buildings. They also painted pictures on paper made from plant fibers and collected them into books.

Indians also used stone to make art. The Maya and Aztec used small pieces of stone to create pictures that are called mosaics. They made statues as well. The Olmec of Mesoamerica used huge pieces of basalt rock to create the oldest large sculptures, or statues, in the Americas. The Maya and Aztec, who followed the Olmec, decorated the outsides of their buildings with flat sculptures.

Many Indians of North America carved smaller statues. Indians of the Northeast and the Plains sculpted elaborate pipes that they used for smoking tobacco. Indians of the Northwest Pacific Coast sculpted with wood. Although they are most known for making totem poles, they carved other objects as well.

Paleo-Indians, who were the first human beings to live in the Americas, often took shelter in caves. They decorated the walls of these ready-made homes with paintings of people and animals. Often they combined these two subjects in hunting scenes. Sometimes they painted symbols or designs. One design that was used in many cave paintings of the Americas was that of a human hand. Another was the spiral. These first artists of the Americas created their work about 11,000 years ago.

American Indian cave artists ground pigments to make their paints. Most of these pigments were naturally occurring minerals that they found in the earth. One of their favorite paints was red ocher. They made it from a mineral called hematite that contains oxidized iron, iron that has combined with oxygen. They also ground charcoal from their fires to make paints. Once the artist had ground the mineral or charcoal into fine particles, he or she mixed it with animal fat, blood, or fish oil.

Early American Indian artists made their pictures in several ways. Some dipped their fingers in the paint that they had made and applied it to the walls or coated their hands with paint and pressed them against the walls to leave an a design. Other rock artists used brushes that they made by fraying, or shredding, the ends of twigs.

Petroglyphs like these that were made in what is now Arizona can be found throughout the Americas. They were made sometime between A.D. 1000 and 1300. *(Library of Congress, Prints and Photographs Division [LC-USZ62-113249])*

Sometimes rock artists stenciled hand designs onto cave walls by putting a hand against the wall and blowing paint around it using a hollow plant stem.

The cave paintings of the Americas that have survived until today are located in dry caves. The most important North American cave painting sites are in Arkansas, the Southwest, California, and Baja California, which is a part of Mexico. Caves that contain many paintings have also been found in Brazil. One of these, Cueva de las Manos, or Cave of the Hands, has been declared a cultural world heritage site by the United Nations.

In addition to using paint to make designs and pictures on rock, early American Indian artists used small pebbles as chipping, or pecking, tools to scratch away at the rock's surface. Chipping tools that have been found in an Arkansas cave were made from pieces of sandstone rock that had been hardened in a fire.

The earliest petroglyphs were made in about 9000 B.C. Like cave paintings, petroglyphs have been found from the southern part of South America to Canada. In North America, many petroglyphs have been found in the Southwest and in Southern California. Petroglyphs have also been found in Minnesota, Kansas, Rhode Island, and in Washington State along the Columbia River. One of the largest collections of petroglyphs in Canada consists of 900 pictures carved into white marble near Toronto, Ontario. These pictures include snakes, birds, turtles, and people, as well as symbols.

Because pictures that have been scratched onto rock are more permanent than drawings made with pigments and charcoal, many petroglyphs have been found on flat rock surfaces outside of caves. Indian people continued to make designs on rocks even after contact with Europeans. For example, Newspaper Rock, near Moab, Utah, contains petroglyphs that were carved in sandstone by Fremont people. (The Fremont people lived in what is now Utah from about A.D. 400 to 1300.) Later Anasazi and Dineh (Navajo) artists added to the rock. Some of the pictures on this rock are of horses. Horses were not introduced to the Southwest by the conquistadores until the 1500s.

WINTER COUNTS

North American Indians of the Plains, who traveled in search of game, developed a portable way to record their history. They painted records of their past onto buffalo hides. These were called winter counts because each winter marked one year that had passed. Some winter counts were made hundreds of years ago. Indian painters copied the designs onto new hides when old hides wore out.

Some of the events that painters of the Plains depicted on hides included good and poor hunting years and arguments with people both inside and outside the tribe. Winter counts also showed the death of leaders and unusual natural events such as big storms and eclipses. Winter counts helped people to remember the past. For this reason the pictures that Indian artists painted on the hides were not detailed. Some of the drawings of animals are very similar to those that had been inscribed on the surface of rocks. Usually elders were the ones who made the hides because people trusted them to pass their knowledge of history to future generations.

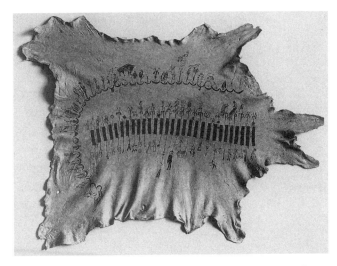

Plains tribes often recorded their history in winter counts, such as this Kiowa painting on buckskin, which was made between 1871 and 1907. (National Archives and Records Administration—College Park/ Photograph No. NWDNS-106-IN-78)

After the arrival of Europeans, American Indian historians began using paper for winter counts. They created pictures with pens, pencils, and watercolor. Ledger books used by military storekeepers and traders became highly prized for recording tribal and personal history.

MURALS

The Maya and the Aztec of Mesoamerica painted murals on the walls of their buildings. The first Mesoamerican mural artists began painting these pictures between A.D. 100 and 250. At first they used mostly red paints and their designs were simple ones. Later they began using many more colors to paint complicated designs and scenes.

The Maya were the most skilled mural painters. Some of the best-preserved Maya murals are those at Bonampak in what is now Chiapas, Mexico. The murals at Bonampak were painted during the Late Classic Period of Maya culture (A.D. 600 to A.D. 900). These vividly colored drawings show the history and culture of the Maya people of this city. They include battle scenes and scenes of a ruler being crowned.

Maya painters used five basic colors—black, blue, red, white, and yellow—for their murals. To obtain them, they used several minerals for paints. These included crushed hematite, carbon, and yellow ocher (mineral iron oxide). Maya painters used cactus juice as a medium for mixing the pigments for their murals. The paints that they made have lasted for more than 1,000 years.

In about A.D. 600 the builders of the city of Teotihuacán in what is now central Mexico covered the walls of much of the city with brilliantly colored murals. Some archaeologists believe that the buildings may have been designed to show off the artwork painted on their walls. Painters made pictures of people, shells, jaguars, birds, fish, water lilies, and many other subjects. When they painted important people in their history, they included headdresses, shields, and rattles in the pictures to identify them.

This drawing of a battle is a facsimile of one made by Ma-Wo-Ma, who was a chief of the Snake Nation (Shoshone). It was published in an 1867 book. *(Alfred J. Miller, Artist/National Archives of Canada/Photograph No. C-013839)*

Maya painters decorated the walls of burial chambers at Bonampak with colorful murals. This picture shows the ruling class. Bonampak is located in the middle of a rain forest near Palenque in what is now Mexico. (© *Philip Baird/www.anthroarcheart.org*)

Seven hundred years later, Aztec painters carried on the mural painting. For the most part, Aztec mural artists decorated the homes of rulers and nobility. Their murals, like those of the Maya and the Teotihuacán artists, recorded the history and religious practices of the people who painted them.

MOSAICS

Mesoamerican artists also decorated the walls of their buildings and the floors with mosaics. They made mosaics by inlaying pieces of colored stone into softer material, such as plaster for walls and sand for floors. The Olmec, whose culture flourished in Mesoamerica from about 1700 B.C. to about 400 B.C., were the first Mesoamericans to develop this art form. They used tiles made from green serpentine rocks that were about the size of present-day cinder blocks. Olmec

Limestone mosaics from a temple in Chichén Itzá, a city founded by the Maya in about A.D. 400 in the Yucatán Peninsula of what is now Mexico. Typically, Mesoamerican builders used large mosaics around the top of buildings, as is the case here. *(Laura Gilpin, Photographer/Library of Congress, Prints and Photographs Division [LCUSZ62-107317])*

artists constructed these mosaics in deep pits and covered them with earth. One such pit found by archaeologists was 16 feet deep and contained a mosaic depicting an Olmec god. Another pit, called "Massive Offerings," was 24 feet deep. The mosaic in this pit contained more than 1,000 tons of green serpentine blocks. Archaeologists do not know why the Olmec buried these mosaics, but they think it may have served a religious purpose.

Maya stonemasons used limestone tiles to decorate the outside walls of many of their buildings. The House of the Governor, which they built in the city of Uxmal between A.D. 600 and 800, covers five acres. The mosaics on the front of the building contained at least 20,000 individually cut stones. The Maya also used mosaics at Chichén Itzá. Often they carved designs into the large tiles that they used to cover buildings. Maya artisans were also experts at making smaller mosaics.

Aztec artists used semiprecious stones for the smaller mosaics that they made. They placed these pictures, made of many tiny pieces of stone, on the inside walls of their palaces. In addition to using stone chips to decorate walls, they also used them for smaller pieces. Mixtec artists, who worked for the Aztec, are well known for the mosaics that they used to cover masks, mirrors, and jewelry. Some of the stones that they used to cover these objects were garnet, mother-of-pearl, seashells, obsidian, jade, and turquoise. To make the mosaics, they cut stones into shape with a string saw, a piece of sturdy twine that was coated with grit. Artisans used cane fibers or fibers from gourd plants to polish the rare stones they used for mosaics. Because these plants contain silica (sand) within their cells, they made excellent abrasives and polishes. Then they glued the small pieces onto a wooden form, using pitch, the sticky sap from trees, as glue.

Ancient goldsmiths of the Andes in South America set shell, turquoise, and other precious and semiprecious gems into gold. They

▲▼▲▼▲▼▲▼▲▼▲▼▲▼▲▼▲▼▲▼▲▼▲▼▲▼▲▼▲

MOSAICS MOVE NORTHWARD

Alta Vista, the center of the Chalchihuites culture, was the site of the first Mesoamerican turquoise mine. The Chalchichuites people lived in the northernmost part of Mesoamerica from about A.D. 200 to about 1200. The artists of this culture made mosaic discs from turquoise, as well as rings, beads, and pendants. They traded these items with the people of Teotihuacán to the south.

In North America the Hohokam of the desert Southwest of what is now Arizona made mosaics perhaps after contact with the Chalchihuites. By A.D. 500 the Hohokam were inlaying turquoise on shells to make necklaces. They traded some of these necklaces to the Anasazi, who lived north of them, and with other neighboring tribes.

▼▲▼▲▼▲▼▲▼▲▼▲▼▲▼▲▼▲▼▲▼▲▼▲▼▲▼▲▼

made hand mirrors with a mosaic on the backside. Moche gold-smiths also placed their mosaic works on beakers (cups without handles), breastplates, and smaller objects, such as ear plugs, a type of earring. Moche culture flourished from 200 B.C. to A.D. 600.

SCULPTURE

Throughout the Americas, Indians made sculptures from stone and wood. Sculptures are three-dimensional carvings. These ranged in size from huge statues to tiny pieces that could be held in the hand. American Indians carved likenesses of people and animals in their environment. They also made religious figures. The stone sculptures have been preserved, but many wooden artworks that Indian artists made have decayed over time.

The Olmec are thought by many art historians to be not only the first but also the greatest stone sculptors in the precontact Americas. They used basalt to make large statues. Although they produced statues that were five to six feet tall, Olmec sculptors are best known for the larger stone pieces that they carved. Some of these big statues weigh more than 20 tons.

The most famous of these statues are the huge carved heads that they made to surround the perimeter of tombs. The Olmec also

The Olmec, whose culture arose in Mesoamerica in about 1700 B.C., created huge sculptures. They carved them from basalt, a volcanic rock. (© *Philip Baird/www.anthroarcheart.org*)

carved life-sized human figures and figures of animals, such as the jaguar. The people that followed the Olmec in Mesoamerica also made sculptures, but these statues were much smaller. Many art historians believe that the Olmec were not only the earliest sculptors in the Americas but that they were also the best.

Many of the large sculptures that the Maya and Aztec artists of Mesoamerica made were used to decorate the outside of buildings. These carvings, which they made from limestone, consisted of panels called friezes. They were sculpted in bas-relief—they were only partly raised from the stone background. Some of them were realistic portrayals of human beings or of gods that looked like human beings that had a special meaning for the people who saw them. Others were geometric designs that were probably meant for decoration. In addition to friezes, the Maya and Aztec sculpted stone pillars.

The Maya made small statues, or figurines, from rock. They created them from clay as well. The Aztec also made smaller statues of stone. They inlaid these with bone, shell, and precious stones. Sometimes they used precious stones, such as jade and obsidian, for their smaller sculptures. They polished these stones to a high shine. Many of these statues were religious in nature.

North American Indians made statues as well. The Indians of the Northwest Pacific Coast carved human and animal figures on wooden poles that they made from tree trunks. They placed these poles in front of their houses or used them as support poles for buildings. The human faces that the Indians carved into these poles were ancestors or people who had once lived in the house. The animals that they carved represented the clans to which the people in the house belonged. Sometimes symbolic animals are called totems. Today these wooden carvings of the Northwest are called totem poles. In addition to creating totem poles, carvers of the Northwest made elaborate bowls, boxes, and rattles from wood. Some Indian people of the Northwest carved wooden masks that they wore dur-

In addition to carving sculptures on buildings, Maya artisans made free-standing stone monuments. This one was found in what is now Guatemala. *(Library of Congress, Prints and Photographs Division [LC-USZ62-97814])*

ing storytelling rituals and religious ceremonies. They painted these masks and sometimes decorated them with feathers and hair to make them appear more lifelike. No two masks were alike.

The Iroquois people of the Northeast also carved wooden masks. Members of the False Face Society, a group of individuals who healed ailments by interpreting dreams, wore them. They wore the masks when they listened to a person's dream and figured out what it meant. Often a dream provided the inspiration for how a mask would look. Iroquois mask artists carved them into living trees, burning and scraping away excess wood. Only when the face was finished did they cut the mask away from the tree trunk. They painted the masks red or black and rubbed them with sunflower oil to make them shine. Often they decorated them with hair.

Indians of the Northeast were excellent sculptors. Apart from masks, they carved figures on small objects such as wooden spoons and pipes. They carved the spoons from hardwood and decorated their handles. Some of the figures they carved were of people and others were of animals, such as turtles or wolves. Carvers of the Northeast and the Southeast made their pipes from soapstone, or steatite, a soft stone that could be easily carved. They shaped the bowls of their pipes into animals, birds, and human faces. They also carved decorative bowls from stone. Indians of the Plains also carved pipes from Catlinite, a soft red stone.

The Inuit people of the Arctic were highly skilled sculptors. The first Inuit carvers lived and worked in about 600 B.C. They were part of the Dorset culture. The materials they used were bone, ivory, and wood. From these they made small figures of animals, such as bears, birds, and whales. They also carved masks. In about A.D. 1000, the Thule people followed them. The Thule were expert tool makers. They focused their carving on objects that they used in their everyday lives. Some of the items that they carved decorations into included harpoon toggles, ivory fish hooks, boxes, and combs. The Inuit believed that good craftsmanship pleased the spirits of the animals who had died to provide the bone and ivory that they carved. Today collectors throughout the world consider their sculptures beautiful works of art.

In the North American Southwest, the Anasazi and Hohokam people carved small animal figures from bone, shell, and stone. They also made figures from clay. The Pueblo people made small statues from cottonwood that represented masked gods that were important in their religion. These carved dolls are called kachinas. Pueblo people decorated them with paint, leather, and feathers. They gave them to their children as educational toys, so that they would learn about

▲▽

A MODERN WINTER COUNT ARTIST

Ambrose Keeble, a member of the Crow Creek Sioux tribe, has been an artist for 15 years. He started by drawing on paper and then painting on canvas, but now he paints on animal hides as well. "That felt like a better way to tell the story of my people," he says. "I paint so that people will remember our history. It is important to make connections between how we lived in the past and how we live today. This is especially true now because so many have chosen to live in cities." He and his family are members of the White Ghost Band of Crow Creek Sioux.

In Keeble's work he combines tradi-tional images, such as eagles, buffalo, and

The circle in the center of this hide painting represents the Sacred Hoop of Life. Around the circle are portraits of famous Indian leaders. Eagles like the ones in this painting have important meaning for the Lakota people. Artist Ambrose Keeble often uses them in his work. *(Kay Marie Porterfield)*

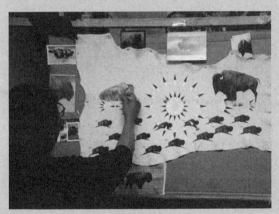

The buffalo provided Indians of the Great Plains with food and hides for clothing and for tipi cover-ings. Because buffalo were such an important part of their lives, they were often portrayed in their art as well. In this modern winter count, Ambrose Keeble combines buffalo symbols with realistic pictures of these animals. *(Kay Marie Porterfield)*

buffalo tracks, with more modern ones. One of his paintings features portraits of his grandfather Buckley Pomani and his great-grandfather Frank Pomani. "My grandfather served in World War I," Keeble says. "Many Indigenous people served in the U.S. Army, but we didn't get citizenship until after the war in 1924. All people, not only Natives, need to remember that part of history."

▽▲

the beliefs of their people. After the Spaniards colonized the Southwest, only the Hopi and the Zuni people continued to make kachinas.

PROTECTING INDIAN ART AND INDIAN ARTISTS

Europeans who came to the Americas collected Indian art because they thought it was odd or curious. In fact, southwestern traders called the paintings and carvings, as well as the pottery and baskets that Indians made, *curios*. In the late 1800s and early 1900s, demand from collectors, including museums, reached a frenzy. Objects were in such demand than that professional grave robbers looted Indian burial sites for artworks. In the Southwest, people called "pot hunters" carelessly dug up the sites of ancient civilizations in order to carry away pottery and other artifacts (art objects left by ancient people) to sell to art collectors and art museums.

To stop this from happening, the U.S. Congress passed the Antiquities Act in 1906. This law was intended to protect artifacts and human remains on land that belonged to the U.S. government. According to the Antiquities Act, the artifacts and the remains of the Indian people on federal land became the property of the U.S. government.

In 1990 the U.S. Congress passed the Native American Graves Protection and Repatriation Act (Public Law 101-601, known as NAGPRA). Since the passage of NAGPRA, museums are required to give Indian ceremonial objects and burial goods, as well as human remains, back to the tribes. Now when burial sites are found on federal land, the U.S. government is required to consult with area tribes to determine who should take care of the artifacts and remains. Pot hunters who are caught on federal lands face big fines and jail sentences today.

Some American Indian artists and craftspeople continue to make art using the traditional styles their ancestors invented before contact with Europeans. Others continue to make silver and turquoise jewelry, beadwork, and quilts—art forms that Indian artists made part of their culture after Europeans arrived in the Western Hemisphere. Still other American Indian artists create works that interpret American Indian beliefs and lifestyles in a more modern artistic expression.

Today Indian art is popular throughout the world. It became so popular that non-Indians began copying Indian designs and claiming that Indians had made the artwork they were trying to sell. The U.S.

Indian Arts and Crafts Act (Public Law 101-644), passed in 1990, makes it illegal for non-Indian artists to claim that their art is Indian art. This protects traditional Indian artists who create beauty with line, color, and shape and who express centuries-old meaning in their work.

GLOSSARY OF ANCIENT CULTURES OF THE AMERICAS

This glossary lists some of the important cultures, empires, and city-states in the Americas before 1492. Many of them existed hundreds or thousands of years before Europeans arrived in the Americas. Archaeologists try to piece together the history of America's ancient people from their buildings and the smaller objects they left behind. They can only make educated guesses based on the artifacts that they find.

The history of ancient America is one of changes. Because of this, modern people often mistakenly think that entire groups of ancient Indian people disappeared. Indian people and their civilizations did not vanish. Governments rose to power, fell, and were replaced by other governments. Sometimes large groups of people moved. They shared ideas with their neighbors and borrowed ideas from them. The Indians who made up civilizations of the past are the ancestors of the Indians of the Americas who are alive today.

Adena   The Adena culture arose along the valleys of the Mississippi and Ohio Rivers and lasted from about 1500 B.C. to A.D. 200. Adena people were farmers and built burial mounds. The Hopewell people followed them.

Anasazi   The Anasazi lived in the southwestern part of what is now the United States in New Mexico, Arizona, Utah, and Colorado. Their culture flourished from about 350 B.C. to

A.D. 1450. They are thought to be the ancestors of modern Pueblo people.

Aztec (Mexica)   The Aztec moved into the Valley of Mexico from the north in about A.D. 1100. Their culture followed that of the Toltec in the region. By 1350 they had expanded their empire and became the dominant state in what became central Mexico. They were the powerful group in that area when the Spaniards arrived. At its largest, the main Aztec city of Tenochtitlán had about 250,000 residents.

Chalchihuite   The Chalchihuite people entered what is now the Sierra Madre of Mexico between A.D. 900 and 1250. They were colonized by the Aztec after the Aztec Empire rose to power. They lived in what was considered the northern frontier of the Aztec Empire.

Chavin   Chavin culture flourished in the fertile river valleys of what is now Peru from about 1000 B.C. to about 200 B.C. The Chavin lived about 1,200 to 2,000 years before the Inca Empire was established.

Chimu   The Chimu civilization lasted from 1100 A.D. to the mid-1400s in what is now Peru. The Chimu state was conquered by the Inca.

Chinchorro   The Chinchorro culture, on the coast of what is now Peru, began in about 5000 B.C. It reached its peak in about 3000 B.C. The Chinchorro are best known for the elaborate ways in which they mummified their dead. They are one of the most ancient cultures to have lived in the region.

Hohokam   The Hohokam culture arose in what is now central and southern Arizona in about 300 B.C. Hohokam people are thought to be the ancestors of the Akimel O'odham (Pima) and the Tohono O'odham (Papago). The Hohokam lived in the Southwest in the same time period as the Anasazi. Their settlements were south of those of the Anasazi.

Hopewell   Hopewell culture arose along the valleys of the Mississippi and Ohio Rivers in about 300 B.C. The Hopewell are considered part of the Mound Builders, along with the Adena people who came before them. They built huge earthworks and flourished until about A.D. 700. They were followed by the Mississippian Culture.

Inca   The Inca established an empire in what is now Peru in about A.D. 1000 and rapidly expanded it. This empire extended from what is now northwest Argentina to parts of what is now Colombia. The Inca Empire was in power when the Spanish conquistador Francisco Pizarro arrived in South America.

Iroquois League (Haudenosaunee)   The Iroquois League, or Haudenosaunee, was an alliance of Northeast tribes established some time between A.D. 1000 and 1400. The tribes included the Oneida, Mohawk, Cayuga, Onondaga, Seneca, and later the Tuscarora.

Maya   The Maya civilization arose in what is now the Yucatán Peninsula of Mexico starting in about 1500 B.C. They did not have a centralized government but instead formed city-states. Maya people also lived in what are now Belize, Guatemala, El Salvador, and Honduras. When the Aztec expanded their empire, they began collecting taxes from the Maya and demanded loyalty to the Aztec Emperor.

Mississippian Culture   The Mississippian Culture arose in about A.D. 1000. Sometimes these people are called temple mound builders. Unlike the Adena and Hopewell people, they built earthworks for temples and ceremonial centers, rather than for burials. They built Cahokia, a city of about 30,000 people, near what is St. Louis, Missouri, today. Mississippian Culture started to weaken in the 1500s, but early French explorers encountered some temple mound builders in the late 1600s.

Mixtec   The Mixtec lived in what is now southern Mexico. Their culture arose in about A.D. 900. The Aztec Empire eventually dominated the Mixtec city-states, but their culture continued to thrive until the arrival of the Spaniards.

Moche   The Moche culture arose on the northern coast of what is now Peru in about 200 B.C. It flourished until about A.D. 600. The Moche were master artists.

Mound Builders   These were American Indians of several cultures who lived in the Mississippi and Ohio River Valleys over a period of time. Some Mound Builders also lived in the Southeast. These people of the Adena, Hopewell, and Mississippian cultures built extensive earthworks.

Nazca   The Nazca people lived in the lowlands of what is now Peru. Their culture arose starting in about 600 B.C. and lasted until about A.D. 900. Later the area where they lived became part of the Inca Empire.

Old Copper Culture   Peoples who lived from about 4000 B.C. to 1500 B.C. in the Great Lakes region of North America. These Indians worked with copper deposits that were close to the surface of the Earth. They made some of the earliest metal tools and objects in the world.

Olmec   The Olmec culture flourished starting in about 1700 B.C. in the coastal lowlands of what is now Mexico. It lasted until about 400 B.C. The Olmec built several cities, including La Venta, which had a population of about 18,000. The Olmec are also known as the Rubber People because they made items from rubber.

Paracas   The Paracas culture arose in the river valleys of what is now Peru in about 1300 B.C. and flourished until about A.D. 20. Paracas people invented many weaving and pottery techniques. A thousand years later, the area where they lived became part of the Inca Empire.

Paleo-Indians   A general term for those who lived before about 4000 B.C. They were the oldest peoples of the Americas. They hunted for their food, killing large mammals, such as the wooly mammoth and the mastodon.

Poverty Point Culture   The people of Poverty Point lived in the Lower Mississippi Valley between 1730 and 1350 B.C. They are a small, distinct group within Mississippian, or Mound Building, Culture.

Teotihuacán   The Teotihuacán culture flourished in the central valley of what is now Mexico from about 1000 B.C. to 900 A.D. At its center was the city-state of Teotihuacán, which was at its strongest from about A.D. 1 to about 650. In A.D. 500 the city was home to between 100,000 and 200,000 people.

Thule   The Thule culture arose in what is now northwestern Alaska between 1,000 and 2,000 years ago. Then it spread to Greenland. Thule people were the ancestors of the Inuit. They are known for their tool-making ability.

Toltec   The Toltec migrated into what is now known as the Valley of Mexico in central Mexico in about A.D. 800. They established their capital at Tula in about 900. About 60,000 people lived in Tula. The Toltec rule lasted until some time in the

1100s, when invading groups attacked and overthrew them. Little is known about the Toltec because the Aztec used the ruins of Tula as a source of building materials for their own monuments.

Zapotec The Zapotec established a city-state south of the Mixtec in what is now southern Mexico. In about 500 B.C. they began building the city of Monte Albán. By A.D. 450, more than 15,000 people lived in Monte Albán. Later this grew to 25,000 people. By about 700 A.D. the Zapotec began moving away from their city. Although their culture remained, the Zapotec no longer had a city-state.

TRIBES ORGANIZED BY CULTURE AREA

North American Culture Areas

ARCTIC CULTURE AREA
Aleut
Inuit

CALIFORNIA CULTURE AREA
Achomawi (Pit River)
Akwaala
Alliklik (Tataviam)
Atsugewi (Pit River)
Bear River
Cahto (Kato)
Cahuilla
Chilula
Chimariko
Chumash
Costanoan (Ohlone)
Cupeño
Diegueño (Ipai)
Esselen
Fernandeño
Gabrieliño
Huchnom
Hupa
Ipai (Diegueño)
Juaneño
Kamia (Tipai)
Karok
Kitanemuk

Konomihu
Lassik
Luiseño
Maidu
Mattole
Miwok
Nicoleño
Nomlaki
Nongatl
Okwanuchu
Patwin (subgroup of Wintun)
Pomo
Salinas
Serrano
Shasta
Sinkyone
Tolowa (Smith River)
Tubatulabal (Kern River)
Vanyume
Wailaki
Wappo
Whilkut
Wintu (subgroup of Wintun)
Wintun
Wiyot
Yahi

Yana
Yokuts
Yuki
Yurok

GREAT BASIN CULTURE AREA
Bannock
Chemehuevi
Kawaiisu
Mono
Paiute
Panamint
Sheepeater (subgroup
of Bannock
and Shoshone)
Shoshone
Snake (subgroup of Paiute)
Ute
Washoe

GREAT PLAINS CULTURE AREA
Arapaho
Arikara
Assiniboine
Atsina (Gros Ventre)
Blackfeet
Blood (subgroup of Blackfeet)
Cheyenne
Comanche
Crow
Hidatsa
Ioway
Kaw
Kichai
Kiowa
Kiowa-Apache
Mandan
Missouria
Omaha
Osage
Otoe
Pawnee
Piegan (subgroup of Blackfeet)

Plains Cree
Plains Ojibway
Ponca
Quapaw
Sarcee
Sioux (Dakota, Lakota, Nakota)
Tawakoni
Tawehash
Tonkawa
Waco
Wichita
Yscani

NORTHEAST CULTURE AREA
Abenaki
Algonkin
Amikwa (Otter)
Cayuga
Chippewa (Ojibway,
Anishinabe)
Chowanoc
Conoy
Coree (Coranine)
Erie
Fox (Mesquaki)
Hatteras
Honniasont
Huron (Wyandot)
Illinois
Iroquois (Haudenosaunee)
Kickapoo
Kitchigami
Lenni Lenape (Delaware)
Machapunga
Mahican
Maliseet
Manhattan (subgroup of Lenni
Lenape or Wappinger)
Massachuset
Mattabesac
Meherrin
Menominee
Miami

Micmac
Mingo (subgroup of Iroquois)
Mohawk
Mohegan
Montauk
Moratok
Nanticoke
Narragansett
Nauset
Neusiok
Neutral (Attiwandaronk)
Niantic
Nipmuc
Noquet
Nottaway
Oneida
Onondaga
Ottawa
Otter (Amikwa)
Pamlico (Pomeiok)
Passamaquoddy
Paugussett
Penacook
Penobscot
Pequot
Pocomtuc
Poospatuck
(subgroup of Montauk)
Potawatomi
Powhatan
Raritan
(subgroup of Lenni Lenape)
Roanoke
Sac
Sakonnet
Secotan
Seneca
Shawnee
Shinnecock
(subgroup of Montauk)
Susquehannock
Tobacco (Petun)

Tuscarora
Wampanoag
Wappinger
Weapemeoc
Wenro
Winnebago (Ho-Chunk)

**NORTHWEST COAST
CULTURE AREA**
Ahantchuyuk
Alsea
Atfalati
Bella Coola
Cathlamet
Cathlapotle
Chastacosta
Chehalis
Chelamela
Chepenafa (Mary's River)
Chetco
Chilluckittequaw
Chimakum
Chinook
Clackamas
Clallam
Clatskanie
Clatsop
Clowwewalla
Comox
Coos
Coquille (Mishikhwutmetunne)
Cowichan
Cowlitz
Dakubetede
Duwamish
Gitskan
Haida
Haisla
Heiltsuk
Kalapuya
Kuitsh
Kwakiutl

Kwalhioqua
Latgawa
Luckiamute
Lumni
Makah
Miluk
Muckleshoot
Multomah (Wappato)
Nanaimo
Nisga
Nisqually
Nooksack
Nootka
Puntlatch
Puyallup
Quaitso (Queets)
Quileute
Quinault
Rogue
Sahehwamish
Samish
Santiam
Seechelt
Semiahmoo
Siletz
Siuslaw
Skagit
Skilloot
Skykomish
Snohomish
Snoqualmie
Songish
Squamish
Squaxon (Squaxin)
Stalo
Swallah
Swinomish
Takelma (Rogue)
Taltushtuntude
Tillamook
Tlingit
Tsimshian

Tututni (Rogue)
Twana
Umpqua
Wappato (Multomah)
Wasco
Watlala (Cascade)
Yamel
Yaquina
Yoncalla

PLATEAU CULTURE AREA
Cayuse
Chelan
Coeur d'Alene
Columbia (Sinkiuse)
Colville
Entiat
Flathead (Salish)
Kalispel
Klamath
Klickitat
Kootenai (Flathead)
Lake (Senijextee)
Lillooet
Methow
Modoc
Molalla
Nez Perce
Ntlakyapamuk (Thompson)
Okanagan
Palouse
Pshwanwapam
Sanpoil
Shuswap
Sinkaietk
Sinkakaius
Skin (Tapanash)
Spokan
Stuwihamuk
Taidnapam
Tenino
Tyigh

Umatilla
Walla Walla
Wanapam
Wauyukma
Wenatchee
Wishram
Yakama

SOUTHEAST CULTURE AREA
Acolapissa
Adai
Ais
Akokisa
Alabama
Amacano
Apalachee
Apalachicola
Atakapa
Avoyel
Bayogoula
Bidai
Biloxi
Caddo
Calusa
Caparaz
Cape Fear
Catawba
Chakchiuma
Chatot
Chawasha (subgroup
of Chitimacha)
Cheraw (Sara)
Cherokee
Chiaha
Chickasaw
Chine
Chitimacha
Choctaw
Congaree
Coushatta
Creek
Cusabo
Deadose

Eno
Eyeish (Ayish)
Griga
Guacata
Guale
Hitchiti
Houma
Ibitoupa
Jeaga
Kaskinampo
Keyauwee
Koroa
Lumbee
Manahoac
Miccosukee
(subgroup of Seminole)
Mobile
Monacan
Moneton
Muklasa
Nahyssan
Napochi
Natchez
Occaneechi
Oconee
Ofo
Okelousa
Okmulgee
Opelousa
Osochi
Pasacagoula
Patiri
Pawokti
Pee Dee
Pensacola
Quinipissa
Santee (Issati)
Saponi
Sawokli
Seminole
Sewee
Shakori
Sissipahaw

Sugeree
Taensa
Tamathli
Tangipahoa
Taposa
Tawasa
Tekesta
Timucua
Tiou
Tohome
Tunica
Tuskegee
Tutelo
Waccamaw
Washa (subgroup of
Chitimacha)
Wateree
Waxhaw
Winyaw
Woccon
Yadkin
Yamasee
Yazoo
Yuchi

SOUTHWEST CULTURE AREA
Akimel O'odham (Pima)
Apache
Coahuiltec
Cocopah
Halchidhoma
Halyikwamai
Havasupai
Hopi
Hualapai
Jumano (Shuman)
Karankawa
Keres (Pueblo Indians)
Kohuana
Maricopa
Mojave
Navajo (Dineh)
Piro (Pueblo Indians)

Pueblo
Quenchan (Yuma)
Shuman (Jumano)
Sobaipuri
Tewa (Pueblo Indians)
Tiwa (Pueblo Indians)
Tohono O'odham (Papago)
Towa (Jemez, Pueblo Indians)
Yaqui
Yavapai
Yuma (Quechan)
Zuni

SUBARCTIC CULTURE AREA
Ahtena (Copper)
Beaver (Tsattine)
Beothuk
Carrier
Chilcotin
Chipewyan
Cree
Dogrib
Eyak
Han
Hare (Kawchottine)
Ingalik
Kolchan
Koyukon
Kutchin
Montagnais
Nabesna
Nahane
Naskapi
Sekani
Slave (Slavery,
Etchaottine)
Tahltan
Tanaina
Tanana
Tatsanottine (Yellowknife)
Tsetsaut
Tutchone (Mountain)

Mesoamerican Culture Area*

Aztec (Mexica-Nahuatl)	Olmec
Chalchiuites	Toltec
Maya	Zapotec
Mixtec	

Circum-Caribbean Culture Area
(West Indies and Portion of Central America)

Arawak	Matagalpa
Boruca	Mosquito
Carib	Paya
Ciboney	Rama
Ciguayo	Silam
Coiba	Sumo
Corobici	Taino
Cuna	Talamanca
Guaymi	Ulva
Guetar	Voto
Jicaque	Yosco
Lucayo	

South American Culture Areas*

ANDEAN CULTURE AREA

Achuari
Aguaruna
Chavin
Chimu
Inca
Jivaro
Mapuche
Moche
Nazca
Quecha

**CENTRAL AND
SOUTHERN CULTURE AREA**

Guarani
Mapuche

**TROPICAL FOREST (AMAZON
BASIN) CULTURE AREA**

Arawak
Carib
Tupi

* These lists do not attempt to include all groups in the area. They do, however, include a mix of ancient and modern peoples.

Appendix

MAPS

North American, Mesoamerican, and Circum-Caribbean Indian Culture Areas

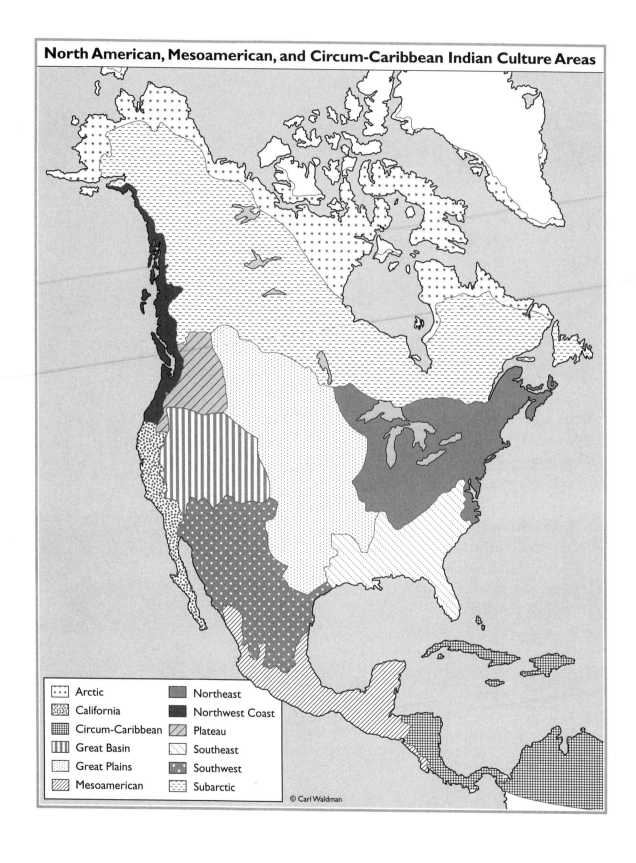

Arctic
California
Circum-Caribbean
Great Basin
Great Plains
Mesoamerican
Northeast
Northwest Coast
Plateau
Southeast
Southwest
Subarctic

© Carl Waldman

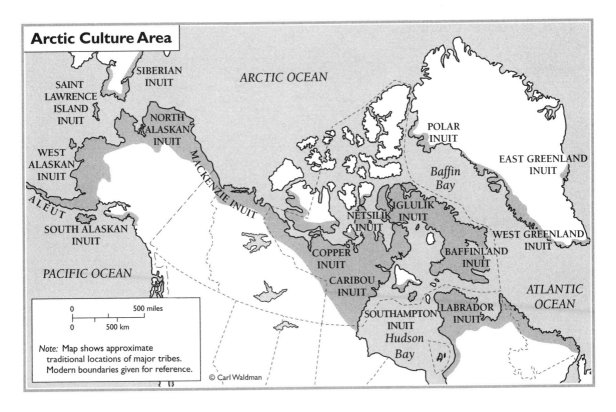

Arctic Culture Area

SIBERIAN INUIT
SAINT LAWRENCE ISLAND INUIT
ARCTIC OCEAN
NORTH ALASKAN INUIT
WEST ALASKAN INUIT
ALEUT
SOUTH ALASKAN INUIT
PACIFIC OCEAN
MACKENZIE INUIT
POLAR INUIT
EAST GREENLAND INUIT
Baffin Bay
NETSILIK INUIT
IGLULIK INUIT
WEST GREENLAND INUIT
COPPER INUIT
BAFFINLAND INUIT
CARIBOU INUIT
ATLANTIC OCEAN
SOUTHAMPTON INUIT
LABRADOR INUIT
Hudson Bay

0   500 miles
0   500 km

Note: Map shows approximate traditional locations of major tribes. Modern boundaries given for reference.

© Carl Waldman

Subarctic Culture Area

KOYUKON
INGALIK
TANAINA TANANA
KUTCHIN
ARCTIC OCEAN
HAN HARE
NABESNA
AHTENA
TUTCHONE
TAGISH
TATSANOTTINE
DOGRIB
TAHLTAN NAHANE
TSETSAUT SLAVE
CHIPEWYAN
Hudson Bay
SEKANI
CARRIER BEAVER
THOMPSON
CHILCOTIN
PACIFIC OCEAN
WESTERN WOODS CREE
SWAMPY CREE
WEST MAIN CREE
EAST MAIN CREE
NASKAPI
MONTAGNAIS
BEOTHUK
CHIPPEWA
ALGONKIN
TÊTE DE BOULE CREE
ATLANTIC OCEAN

0   500 miles
0   500 km

Note: Map shows approximate traditional locations of major tribes. Modern boundaries given for reference.

© Carl Waldman

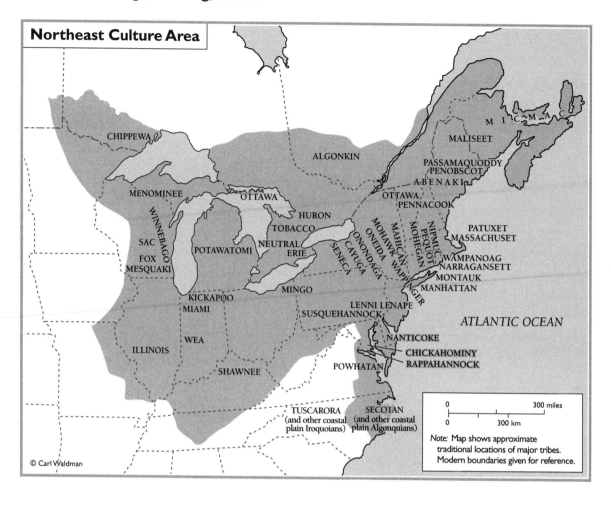

Northeast Culture Area

CHIPPEWA

MENOMINEE

ALGONKIN

MALISEET

PASSAMAQUODDY
PENOBSCOT

ABENAKI

OTTAWA

OTTAWA
PENNACOOK

WINNEBAGO

HURON

TOBACCO

NIPMUC
PEQUOT
MOHEGAN

PATUXET
MASSACHUSET

SAC

NEUTRAL
ERIE

MOHAWK
MAHICAN
ONEIDA
ONONDAGA
CAYUGA
SENECA
WAPPINGER

WAMPANOAG
NARRAGANSETT

FOX
MESQUAKI

POTAWATOMI

MINGO

MONTAUK
MANHATTAN

KICKAPOO

MIAMI

LENNI LENAPE

SUSQUEHANNOCK

ATLANTIC OCEAN

WEA

ILLINOIS

NANTICOKE

CHICKAHOMINY
RAPPAHANNOCK

SHAWNEE

POWHATAN

M I C M A C

TUSCARORA
(and other coastal
plain Iroquoians)

SECOTAN
(and other coastal
plain Algonquians)

0   300 miles

0   300 km

Note: Map shows approximate
traditional locations of major tribes.
Modern boundaries given for reference.

© Carl Waldman

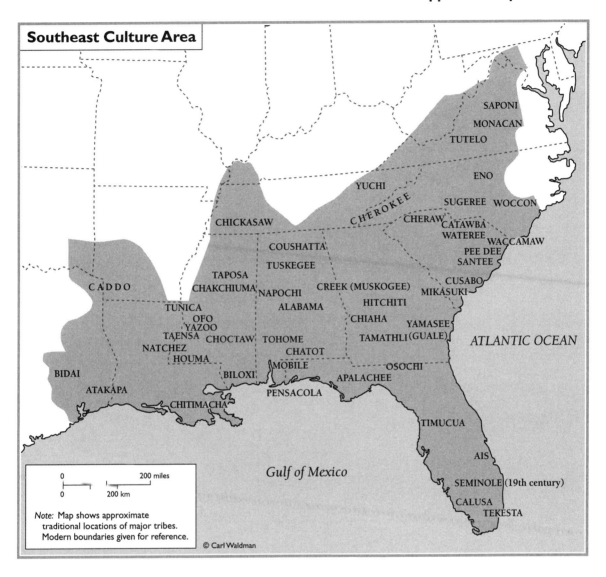

Southeast Culture Area

SAPONI
MONACAN
TUTELO
ENO
YUCHI
SUGEREE   WOCCON
CHEROKEE
CHICKASAW
CHERAW
CATAWBA
WATEREE
WACCAMAW
COUSHATTA
PEE DEE
TUSKEGEE
SANTEE
TAPOSA
CUSABO
CHAKCHIUMA
NAPOCHI
CREEK (MUSKOGEE)
MIKASUKI
CADDO
HITCHITI
TUNICA
ALABAMA
OFO
CHIAHA
YAZOO
YAMASEE
TAENSA
CHOCTAW   TOHOME
TAMATHLI (GUALE)
NATCHEZ
CHATOT
HOUMA
BIDAI
BILOXI
MOBILE
OSOCHI
ATAKAPA
PENSACOLA
APALACHEE
CHITIMACHA

ATLANTIC OCEAN

TIMUCUA

AIS

Gulf of Mexico

SEMINOLE (19th century)

CALUSA
TEKESTA

0 ⊢———⊣ 200 miles
0 ⊢———⊣ 200 km

Note: Map shows approximate
traditional locations of major tribes.
Modern boundaries given for reference.

© Carl Waldman

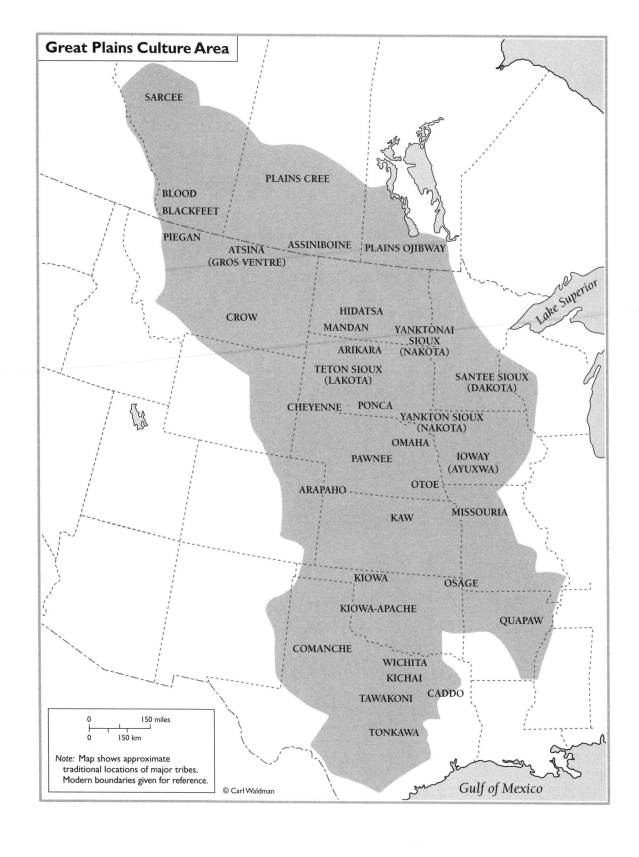

Great Plains Culture Area

SARCEE

PLAINS CREE

BLOOD
BLACKFEET

PIEGAN

ATSINA
(GROS VENTRE)

ASSINIBOINE   PLAINS OJIBWAY

Lake Superior

CROW

HIDATSA

MANDAN

ARIKARA

TETON SIOUX
(LAKOTA)

YANKTONAI
SIOUX
(NAKOTA)

SANTEE SIOUX
(DAKOTA)

CHEYENNE   PONCA

YANKTON SIOUX
(NAKOTA)

OMAHA

PAWNEE

IOWAY
(AYUXWA)

ARAPAHO

OTOE

MISSOURIA

KAW

KIOWA

OSAGE

KIOWA-APACHE

QUAPAW

COMANCHE

WICHITA

KICHAI

TAWAKONI   CADDO

TONKAWA

Gulf of Mexico

0   150 miles

0   150 km

Note: Map shows approximate
traditional locations of major tribes.
Modern boundaries given for reference.

© Carl Waldman

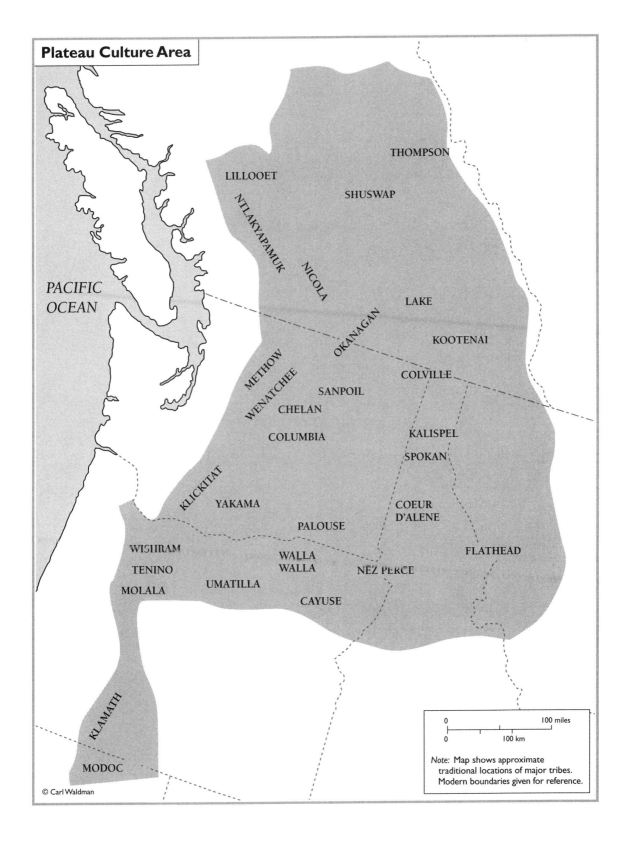

Plateau Culture Area

PACIFIC
OCEAN

THOMPSON

LILLOOET

NTLAKYAPAMUK

SHUSWAP

NICOLA

LAKE

OKANAGAN

KOOTENAI

METHOW

COLVILLE

WENATCHEE

SANPOIL

CHELAN

COLUMBIA

KALISPEL

SPOKAN

KLICKITAT

YAKAMA

COEUR
D'ALENE

PALOUSE

WISHRAM

WALLA
WALLA

FLATHEAD

TENINO

NEZ PERCE

MOLALA

UMATILLA

CAYUSE

KLAMATH

0   100 miles

0   100 km

Note: Map shows approximate
traditional locations of major tribes.
Modern boundaries given for reference.

MODOC

© Carl Waldman

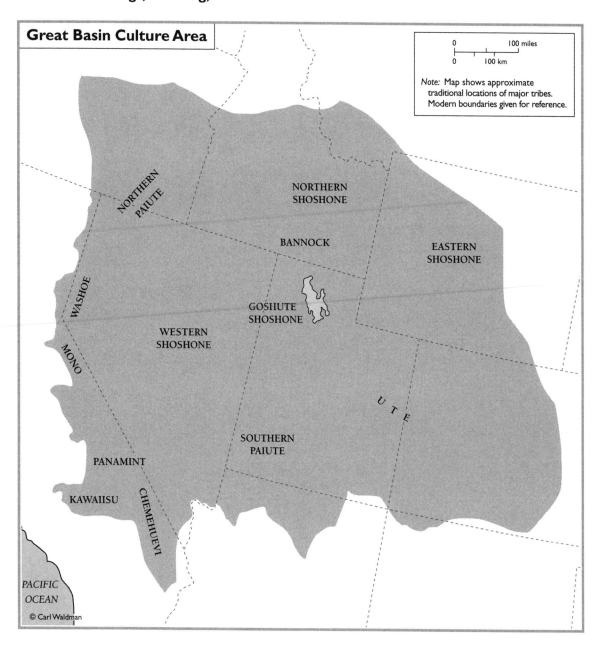

Great Basin Culture Area

0 ——— 100 miles
0 ——— 100 km

Note: Map shows approximate traditional locations of major tribes. Modern boundaries given for reference.

NORTHERN PAIUTE

NORTHERN SHOSHONE

BANNOCK

EASTERN SHOSHONE

WASHOE

GOSHUTE SHOSHONE

WESTERN SHOSHONE

MONO

U T E

SOUTHERN PAIUTE

PANAMINT

KAWAIISU

CHEMEHUEVI

PACIFIC OCEAN

© Carl Waldman

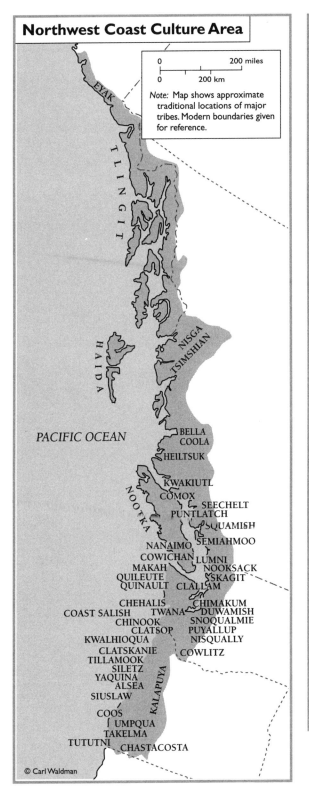

Northwest Coast Culture Area

0   200 miles

0   200 km

Note: Map shows approximate traditional locations of major tribes. Modern boundaries given for reference.

EYAK

TLINGIT

HAIDA

NISGA

TSIMSHIAN

PACIFIC OCEAN

BELLA COOLA

HEILTSUK

KWAKIUTL

COMOX

NOOTKA

SEECHELT

PUNTLATCH

SQUAMISH

NANAIMO   SEMIAHMOO

COWICHAN

LUMNI

MAKAH   NOOKSACK

QUILEUTE   SKAGIT

QUINAULT   CLALLAM

CHEHALIS   CHIMAKUM

COAST SALISH   TWANA   DUWAMISH

CHINOOK   SNOQUALMIE

CLATSOP   PUYALLUP

KWALHIOQUA   NISQUALLY

CLATSKANIE   COWLITZ

TILLAMOOK

SILETZ

YAQUINA

ALSEA

SIUSLAW

KALAPUYA

COOS

UMPQUA

TAKELMA

TUTUTNI   CHASTACOSTA

© Carl Waldman

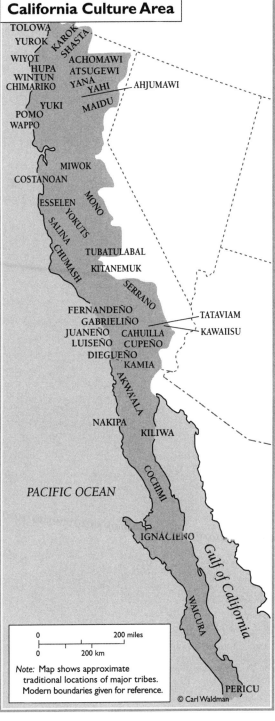

California Culture Area

TOLOWA   KAROK

YUROK   SHASTA

WIYOT   ACHOMAWI

HUPA   ATSUGEWI

WINTUN   YANA

CHIMARIKO   YAHI   AHJUMAWI

YUKI   MAIDU

POMO

WAPPO

MIWOK

COSTANOAN

ESSELEN

YOKUTS

MONO

SALINA

CHUMASH

TUBATULABAL

KITANEMUK

SERRANO

FERNANDEÑO   TATAVIAM

GABRIELIÑO   KAWAIISU

JUANEÑO   CAHUILLA

LUISEÑO   CUPEÑO

DIEGUEÑO

KAMIA

AKWA'ALA

NAKIPA

KILIWA

PACIFIC OCEAN

COCHIMI

IGNACIEÑO

Gulf of California

WAICURA

Note: Map shows approximate traditional locations of major tribes. Modern boundaries given for reference.

PERICU

© Carl Waldman

Southwest Culture Area

HUALAPAI
HAVASUPAI
HOPI
JICARILLA APACHE
MOJAVE
NAVAJO
HALCHIDHOMA
TIWA
YAVAPAI
TOWA   TEWA
MARICOPA
ZUNI
PECOS
YUMA
KERES
TIWA
COCOPAH
PIRO
WESTERN APACHE
TOHONO O'ODHAM
MIMBRENO APACHE
CHIRICAHUA APACHE
MESCALERO APACHE
AKIMEL O'ODHAM
SUMA
OPATA
JUMANO
SERI
CAHITA   JOVA   CONCHO
LIPAN APACHE
Gulf of California
YAQUI
TEPAHUE
TARAHUMARA
KARANKAWA
VAVROHIO
MAYO
TOBOSO
ZOE
COMANITO
NIO
COAHUILTEC
GUASAVE
LAGUNERO
TEPEHUAN
ZACATEC
BOCALOS
JANAMBRE
PISONES
NEGRITO
Gulf of Mexico
PACIFIC OCEAN
HUICHOL
TEPECANO
GUACHICHIL
GUAMARES
JONAZ
COLOTLAN
TEUL
PAME
TAMAULIPEC

0   150 miles
0   150 km

Note: Map shows approximate
traditional locations of major tribes.
Modern boundaries given for reference.

© Carl Waldman

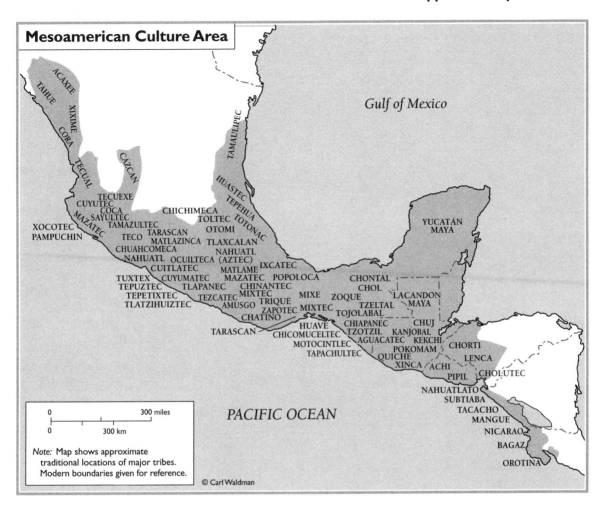

Mesoamerican Culture Area

Gulf of Mexico

ACAXEE
TAHUE
XIXIME
CORA
TECUAL
CAZCAN

TAMAULIPEC

HUASTEC
TEPEHUA
TOTONAC

TECUEXE
CUYUTEC
COCA
SAYULTEC
CHICHIMECA
TOLTEC
TAMAZULTEC
OTOMI
XOCOTEC
MAZATEC
TARASCAN
PAMPUCHIN
TECO
MATLAZINCA
TLAXCALAN
CHUAHCOMECA
NAHUATL
NAHUATL
OCUILTECA
(AZTEC)
CUITLATEC
MATLAME
IXCATEC
TUXTEX
CUYUMATEC
MAZATEC
POPOLOCA
TEPUZTEC
TLAPANEC
CHINANTEC
TEPETIXTEC
MIXTEC
MIXE
ZOQUE
TEZCATEC
TLATZIHUIZTEC
AMUSGO
TRIQUE
ZAPOTEC
MIXTEC
CHATINO
HUAVE
CHIAPANEC
TARASCAN
CHICOMUCELTEC
TZOTZIL
MOTOCINTLEC
AGUACATEC
TAPACHULTEC
QUICHE
XINCA
ACHI
PIPIL

YUCATÁN
MAYA

CHONTAL
CHOL
LACANDON
TZELTAL
MAYA
TOJOLABAL
CHUJ
KANJOBAL
KEKCHI
CHORTI
POKOMAM
LENCA
CHOLUTEC

NAHUATLATO
SUBTIABA
TACACHO
MANGUE
NICARAO
BAGAZ
OROTINA

PACIFIC OCEAN

0		300 miles
0		300 km

Note: Map shows approximate
traditional locations of major tribes.
Modern boundaries given for reference.

© Carl Waldman

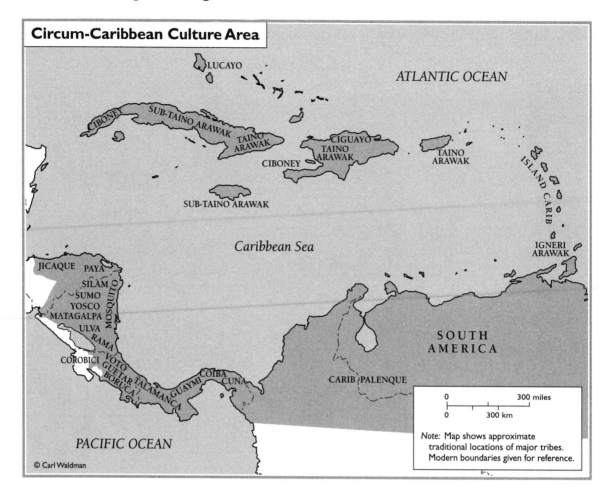

Circum-Caribbean Culture Area

LUCAYO

ATLANTIC OCEAN

CIBONEY

SUB-TAINO ARAWAK

TAINO ARAWAK

CIGUAYO TAINO ARAWAK

CIBONEY

CIBONEY

TAINO ARAWAK

ISLAND CARIB

SUB-TAINO ARAWAK

Caribbean Sea

IGNERI ARAWAK

JICAQUE PAYA

SILAM

SUMO

YOSCO

MATAGALPA

ULVA

MOSQUITO

RAMA

COROBICI

YOTO

GUETAR

BORUCA

TALAMANCA

GUAYMI

COIBA

CUNA

SOUTH
AMERICA

CARIB PALENQUE

0   300 miles

0   300 km

PACIFIC OCEAN

© Carl Waldman

Note: Map shows approximate
traditional locations of major tribes.
Modern boundaries given for reference.

South American Culture Areas

CIRCUM-CARIBBEAN

CARIB
PALENQUE

TUPI
ARAWAK

AGUARUNA
ACHUARI
JIVARO

CARIB

ARAWAK

TUPI

CHIMU

INCA

TROPICAL FOREST

ANDEAN

EASTERN
HIGHLANDS

GUARANI

GUARANI

CENTRAL AND SOUTHERN

MAPUCHE

PAMPAS

TIERRA DEL FUEGO

ANDEAN	Culture areas
PAMPAS	Regions
MAPUCHE	Tribes and peoples
——————	Approximate culture area boundaries
··············	Approximate regional boundaries

0   800 miles

0   800 km

Note: See the Circum-Caribbean map for the entire scope of the culture area.

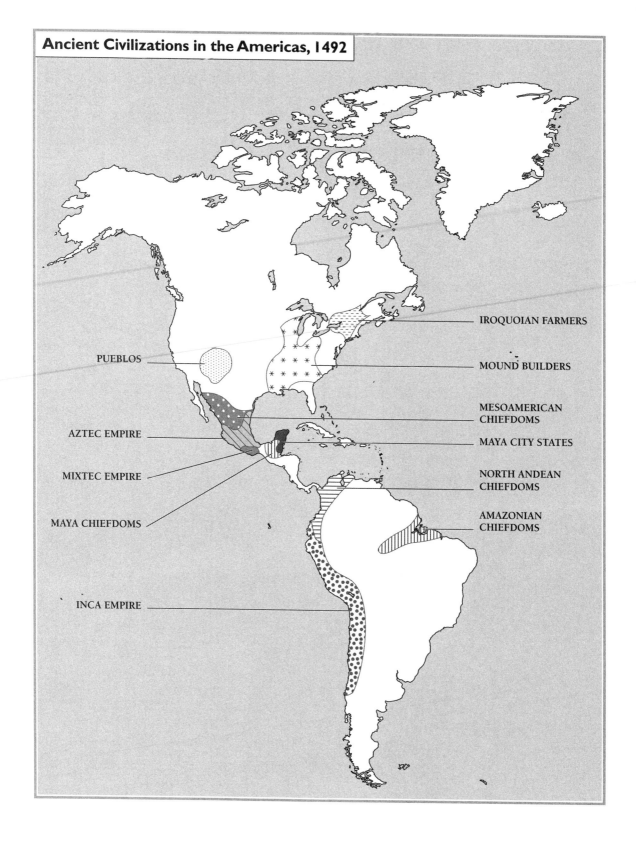

Ancient Civilizations in the Americas, 1492

IROQUOIAN FARMERS

PUEBLOS

MOUND BUILDERS

MESOAMERICAN CHIEFDOMS

AZTEC EMPIRE

MAYA CITY STATES

MIXTEC EMPIRE

NORTH ANDEAN CHIEFDOMS

MAYA CHIEFDOMS

AMAZONIAN CHIEFDOMS

INCA EMPIRE

FURTHER READING

Baquedano, Elizabeth. *Aztec, Inca and Maya*. New York: DK Publishing, 2000.

Carrasco, David. *Daily Life of the Aztecs: Keepers of the Sun and Moon*. Westport, Conn.: Greenwood Press, 1998.

Goodchild, Peter. *Survival Skills of the North American Indians*. 2d ed. Chicago: Chicago Review Press, 1999.

Keoke, Emory, and Kay Marie Porterfield. *Encyclopedia of American Indian Contributions to the World: 15,000 Years of Inventions and Innovation*. New York: Facts On File, Inc., 2002.

Liptak, Karen. *North American Indian Survival Skills*. New York: Franklin Watts, 1990.

Lourie, Peter. *Lost Treasure of the Inca*. Honesdale, Pa.: Boyds Mills Press, 1999.

Malpass, Michael A. *Daily Life in the Inca Empire*. Westport, Conn.: Greenwood Press, 2002.

Miller, Mary Ellen. *The Art of Mesoamerica: From Olmec to Aztec*. 3d ed. New York: Thames & Hudson, 2001.

Montgomery, David. *Native American Crafts and Skills: A Fully Illustrated Guide to Wilderness Living and Survival*. Guilford, Conn.: The Lyons Press, 2000.

Murdoch, David. *Eyewitness: North American Indians*. New York: DK Publishers, 2000.

Penney, David, and George Horse Capture. *North American Indian Art*. New York: Thames & Hudson, 2004.

Sharer, Robert J. *Daily Life in Maya Civilization*. Westport, Conn.: Greenwood Press, 2002.

Steele, Philip. *The Aztec News*. Cambridge, Mass.: Candlewick Press, 2000.

Steedman, Scott. *How Would You Survive As an American Indian?* New York: Franklin Watts, 1997.

Stone-Miller, Rebecca. *Art of the Andes: From Chaving to Inca.* 2d ed. New York: Thames & Hudson, 2001.

Wolfson, Evelyn. *From Abenaki to Zuni: A Dictionary of Native American Tribes.* New York: Walker Publishing Co., Inc., 1988.

Wood, Marian. *Ancient America: Cultural Atlas for Young People, Revised Edition.* New York: Facts On File, Inc., 2003.

INDEX

Page numbers in *italics* indicate photographs. Page numbers in **boldface** indicate box features. Page numbers followed by *m* indicate maps. Page numbers followed by *g* indicate glossary entries. Page numbers followed by *t* indicate time line entries.